MOON TEMPLE ORACLE

YOUR PERSONAL PORTAL TO THE COSMOS

SUZY CHERUB
ARTWORK BY LAILA SAVOLAINEN

BLUE ANGEL®
PUBLISHING

Copyright © 2024 Suzy Cherub
Artwork Copyright © 2024 Laila Savolainen

All rights reserved. Other than for personal use, no part of these cards or this book may be reproduced in any way, in whole or part, without the written consent of the copyright holder or publisher. This publication is intended for spiritual and emotional guidance only. The content is not intended to replace medical assistance or treatment. The views and opinions expressed by the author, both within and outside of this publication, do not necessarily reflect the views of the publisher.

Published by Blue Angel Publishing®
10 Trafford Court, Wheelers Hill,
Victoria, Australia 3150
E-mail: info@blueangelonline.com
Website: www.blueangelonline.com

Edited by Jules Sutherland and Peter Loupelis

Blue Angel is a registered trademark of Blue Angel Gallery Pty Ltd.

ISBN: 978-1-922574-22-0

NEW MOON

The night is dark and silent
No silver light to guide my way
But I do not fear the shadows
I embrace the mystery

The new moon is a promise
A chance to start anew
To plant the seeds of my dreams
And watch them grow and bloom

The new moon is a blessing
A gift from the Divine
To remind me of my potential
And the power that is mine

The new moon is a portal
A doorway to the unknown
To explore the hidden realms
And discover what I own
The new moon is a friend
A companion in the dark
To inspire me and challenge me
And ignite my inner spark

DEDICATION

For my wild moon child and high priestess daughter Bec,
my free-spirited, imaginative and creative son Steven,
my beloved Tony, adored father and nonno,
my curious and magical grandchildren, Noah and Hugo,
my second son and daughter, Matthew and Elise,
my fur baby Pablo,

For my soul family, ancestral and spiritual guides, teachers
and the luminous moon divinities,
For the traditional custodians and First Nations peoples of the
cultures included herein,

For the artistic brilliance of Laila,
and the soulful creativity of the Blue Angel Publishing family.

I love you.
I thank you!

ACKNOWLEDGEMENT

I would like to acknowledge the wise and wonderful Walbunja people of the Yuin nation as the traditional owners of the land that I work and live on, and pay my respect to elders past, present and emerging.

I would also like to honour and sincerely thank the diverse range of ancient custodians, lunar deities and present-day cultures and lands represented in this body of work. I honourably hope I did you justice.

Sincere thanks,
—Suzy

CONTENTS

WELCOME TO THE MOON TEMPLE ORACLE   11
    The Power and Phases of the Moon   12
    What Is a Moon Temple?   15
    How to Lightwork with the *Moon Temple Oracle*   18
    Oracle Card Readings — Groundwork   21
    Moon Temple Oracle Card Layouts   25

MUSINGS FROM THE MOON – CARD MEANINGS

<u>Abuk's Moon Temple: South Sudan and Ethiopia</u>   40
    1. Instinct — Full Moon   42
    2. Freedom — Balsamic Moon   46
    3. Seed — New Moon   51
    4. Strength — First Quarter Moon   55

<u>Aelua's Moon Temple: Portugal</u>   60
    5. Mystery — Full Moon   62
    6. Patience — New Moon   66
    7. Gratitude — Full Moon   71
    8. Protection — Gibbous Moon   75

<u>Cerridwen's Moon Temple: Celtic</u>   80
    9. Fate — Waxing Crescent Moon   82
    10. Innocence — New Moon   86
    11. Prowess — Full Moon   90
    12. Rebirth — Dark Moon   94

Diana's Moon Temple: Rome **98**
13. Hunt — Gibbous Moon **100**
14. Fertility — New Moon **104**
15. Truth — Third Quarter Moon **108**
16. Crossroad — Triple Goddess Moon **112**

Hanwi's Moon Temple: Dakota (Očeti Šakowiŋ) **116**
17. Shelter — Full Moon **118**
18. Refuge — Disseminating Moon **122**
19. Rhythm — All Moon Phases **126**
20. Insight — New Moon **130**

Hina's Moon Temple: Hawai'i **134**
21. Culmination — Balsamic Moon **136**
22. Transition — All Moon Phases **140**
23. Design — New Moon **144**
24. Journey — Waxing Moon **148**

Inanna's Moon Temple: Sumer **152**
25. Sensuality — Disseminating Moon **154**
26. Shadow — Dark Moon **158**
27. Temple — Full Moon **162**
28. Vision — New Moon **166**

Jacira's Moon Temple: Brazil **170**
29. Creation — Full Moon **172**
30. Birth — New Moon **176**
31. Grace — Waxing Moon **180**
32. Tears — Balsamic Moon **184**

Máni's Moon Temple: Norse **188**
33. Chariot — Waxing Crescent **190**
34. Illumination — Sun and Moon **194**
35. Impact — Lunar Eclipse **198**
36. Head-to-Head — Full Moon **202**

Mayari's Moon Temple: Philippines **206**
37. Love — Blood Full Moon **208**
38. Progress — First Quarter Moon **212**
39. Conquest — Third Quarter Moon **216**
40. Beauty — Full Moon **220**

Phoebe's Moon Temple: Greece **224**
41. Wisdom — Balsamic Moon **226**
42. Intellect — Third Quarter Moon **231**
43. Cycle — All Moon Phases **235**
44. Reflection — Gibbous Moon **240**

ABOUT THE AUTHOR 246
ABOUT THE ARTIST 249

THE CALL
OF THE MOON

She calls to you every night,
Her moonlight is so bright,
She calls to you every night,
She is the eternal light.

WELCOME
TO THE
MOON TEMPLE
●●●◖ ORACLE ◗●●●

WISHING YOU A GLOWY WELCOME, MOON LOVER.

IF YOU HAVE BEEN GUIDED TO THIS DECK, THERE IS A GOOD chance you are a devoted selenophile. Selenophile translates to 'moon lover', and derives from the Greek words *selene*, meaning 'moon' and *phile*, meaning 'lover'.

The *Moon Temple Oracle* has been created for you and all selenophiles alike.

May the glow of the moon show you the way, even on your darkest day.

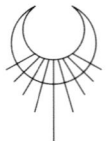

THE POWER AND PHASES OF THE MOON

As the brightest and most majestic orb in our dazzling evening sky, the moon symbolises the rhythm of time, natural cycles and seasons of creation. It ensures the earth is balanced on its axis, stabilising the climate, wheeling the ocean tides, and creating a rhythm and guiding light that has steered souls for eons and eons.

Representing the Divine Feminine in all her celebrated aspects, the moon teaches us how to live in flow with our own cyclic nature.

Women and menstruating people have a special spiritual connection with the moon. The moon takes 28 days to complete its sequence and the feminine cycle takes around the same time. In many traditions a woman's bleeding period is referred to as their 'moontime'. Even the words 'menstruation' or *menses* originate from the connection between the moon and month.

The phases of the lunar cycle align with the life stages of a woman, the phases of the menstrual cycle, and nature's seasons:

DARK MOON

Life Stage/Archetype: Crone
Menstrual Phase: Period
Season: Winter
Moon Goddess: Cerridwen

WAXING MOON

Life Stage/Archetype: Maiden
Menstrual Phase: Follicular
Season: Spring
Moon Goddess: Blodeuwedd, Diana

FULL MOON

Life Stage/Archetype: Mother
Menstrual Phase: Ovulation
Season: Summer
Moon Goddess: Jacira

WANING MOON

Life Stage/Archetype: Wise Woman or Queen
Menstrual Phase: Luteal
Season: Autumn
Moon Goddess: Inanna

Many spiritual philosophies identify our profound union with the moon and recognise that spiritual energy is more powerful when initiated at different times in the lunar cycle. Moon magic comes in many forms — a ceremony, wish, affirmation, verse, chant or any combination that aligns to the current lunar phase. You can use a variety of divination tools, like these oracle cards, as well as candles, crystals and essential oil blends to enhance the manifestation power of the moon.

When you harness the mystery of the moon and employ spiritual practices aligned to the current moon phase, it amplifies your intention and manifestations. For example, the New Moon signifies the beginning of a fresh lunar cycle. It is the perfect time to set new intentions and start projects. In contrast, the Full Moon is a time of releasing, welcoming closure and tying up any loose ends. Intuitive sensitivity is also magnified under the Full Moon which makes it an especially powerful time for spiritual divination.

WHAT IS A MOON TEMPLE?

MOONLIT TEMPLES, NATURAL CAVERNS AND PYRAMIDS dedicated to lunar deities are scattered throughout history and present-day times. Time-honoured traditions, rituals and divination infuse these natural wonders, ethereal temples and sacred sites with everlasting moondust.

A temple can be a place of worship, a dedicated sacred space, or any spiritual shrine that houses a divine essence, and their set of principles and mythology. It can be a physical space or, in the case of the *Moon Temple Oracle*, a metaphorical one embodying the energy, mythologies and devotion of a lunar deity.

Each moon temple series within the *Moon Temple Oracle* is represented by a lunar deity from an ancient or living culture around the world, along with their corresponding legends and spiritual symbology.

While there is not necessarily an actual lunar temple, shrine or sanctuary in physical form for each deity, their moon temples are given life through their stories, myths and devotion. Everything has an energetic imprint, spirit and vibration, especially when imbued with conscious intention, prayer and devoted spiritual practice.

Eleven different moon temples form the basis of this oracle, and each temple is home to four cards and card messages. You can find in-depth information and guidance about each specific moon temple—its origins, traditions, folklore, etc.—at the start of each four-card section of the guidebook.

As the author, it is my intention to reawaken the literal and metaphorical moon temples on Earth, and within each of us. Each moon's divinity originates from a culture with a rich and intricate cultural heritage. Please note that the guidance related to each deity is the result of my own intuitive impressions and research and does not always reflect the pre-existing lore or myth surrounding the peoples and cultures of those lands.

With deep respect,
—Suzy

IGNITE YOUR LIGHT

*Lunar light is aglow within your soul,
a bright orb of dazzling light inspires,
and ignites insight,
creative spark and enchanted ways,
shimmering like stars in the night sky,
come home to your moon temple,
soar into the mystique,
in lunar love, grace and wisdom,
I bow to you,
Thank you!*

HOW TO LIGHTWORK WITH THE *MOON TEMPLE ORACLE*

You may wish to consecrate your shiny new deck by leaving it out in the cleansing moonlight overnight and following the ritual below.

MOON INVITATION — CONSECRATING YOUR DECK

With potent intention, focus on spiritual devotion and dedicate the *Moon Temple Oracle* card deck by infusing it with sparkly moonlight:

Cradle the deck in both hands, then energetically blow shimmering moondust into the oracle cards to consecrate for higher service to yourself and others.

Take three deep sacred breaths, lift the deck to the moon and

imprint with lunar magic.
Recite the following blessing with intention, feeling a deep knowing within your soul:

*I am a luminary! Ethereal insights flow freely to me.
May it be so. Thank you!*

Invoke the moon guides of the Moon Temple Oracle to enlighten your oracle messages, using the chant below.

Oh, my lunar love, create in me a pure heart, renew a conscious calm within me. May it be so. Thank you!

CELESTIAL UNION — GETTING TO KNOW YOUR DECK

IT HELPS TO BUILD A STRONG RELATIONSHIP WITH YOUR DECK BY using it regularly, so you get a sense for how it works for you. To underpin your psychic confidence and lunar knowledge, you may wish to learn and intuit one card a day by going through the entire deck from start to finish. Once you know the higher meanings, you can delve deeper with your own intuition to make even more sense of the cards. As you get to know each card intimately by reading and understanding the universal meanings, this will reinforce your self-assurance, strengthen your psychic powers and connect you with the moon guides for mystical support.

ORACLE CARD READINGS — GROUNDWORK

PREPARE YOUR SPACE

First, set the scene by either lighting some candles, burning incense or diffusing essential oils. Then cleanse your space with scented smoke, bells, singing bowls or an energetic spray, or simply go to a peaceful place where you feel serene and won't be disturbed. You may wish to recite this chant:

Oh, lunar light, clear and charge this space, ablaze with rays of divine and magical essence. May it be so. Thank you!

PREPARE YOURSELF

ONCE YOUR SPACE IS READY, CENTRE YOURSELF AND ALIGN WITH the moon so that your energy is clear of interference. Even in the daytime, the moon is glowing up there somewhere. Look and reach up to the expansive sky and sense glimmers of the moon shining down on you.

You can do this by taking some harmonising breaths and imagining for a few moments that rays of moonlight are cleansing and activating your aura. See your spirit aglow with dazzling moonshine. Visualise moonbeams aligning you to the magnification power of the moon. Repeat the following chant with strong intent and real heart:

Oh, lunar divine, cleanse and imbue my aura with moonbeams of serenity and celestial wisdom. May it be so. Thank you!

GUIDEBOOK AND CARD OVERVIEW

THIS GUIDEBOOK REVEALS HOW TO INTUIT THE CARDS AND lightwork with them to create, plan and prophesise your future.

Consciously conjure up lunar magic with the divine assistance of your chosen moon guide, and their unified essence, moon phase and spiritual meaning. Layered magic is congruent energies uniting with deliberate focus to activate your intuition and manifestation powers. Every oracle meaning has multifaceted magic that aligns harmoniously to the overall vision. Consecrate your moon magic with powerful intention, aligned affirmations, potent rituals, spell chants and poetry in motion.

The card structure and guidebook layout have a magical synergy that ties all the subheadings beautifully together to make spiritual and practical sense.

Each Oracle Card Includes …
Each card message contains the following elements to support you to connect with the card's guidance:

Main Word: A core word that indicates the root meaning of the oracle card.

Affirmation: A short and compelling declaration to help you tap into your inner power and inspire positive thoughts.

Moonlit Codewords: Three encrypted words, to support the opening of psychic portals for swift, intuitive awareness into the overall energy and high-level connotation of each card.

Moonbeam Insight: A lunar-inspired revelation, which is a more comprehensive card meaning that weaves spiritual guidance, supportive advice and a psychic forecast to lead you in the direction of your glistening dreams.

Moon Guide: A matching lunar deity with special gifts to guide you to attain your greatest potential on Earth.

Moon Phase: Every unique moon rotation presents you with an opportunity to manifest, reflect, take action or rest.

Moon Ritual: A concise, yet powerful lunar ceremony to align you to your chosen oracle card, with corresponding moon magic to craft miracles in your life.

Moon Spell Chant: The intentional chanting of words cast a magical spell. This mystical mantra helps you consciously craft wonders in your sphere.

Artist Prose: Finally, the artist, Laila Savolainen has written some inspired poetry and artistic impressions to accompany each card.

Allow the moon, lunar deities and your own higher self to guide you as you use the *Moon Temple Oracle* in a way that brings the greatest benefit to you and the whole globe.

May you moon-dance through the mystique and mysteries of life!

MOON TEMPLE ORACLE CARD LAYOUTS

AN ORACLE CARD READING CAN BE DONE EITHER BY INTUITIVELY drawing any card that speaks to you or laying cards down in a chosen spread. A card layout provides a high-level structural framework to give your reading a focused intention and many layers of meaning.

Below are some optional *Moon Temple Oracle* spreads that you can use. You can either select the card layout below that is the most applicable to you at any time, or you may be spontaneously guided to simply pull a card or two and read intuitively.

Whenever you need to make a decision, or you're purely looking for inspiration, you can just pick a card and let the moon guide you. There is no right or wrong, so trust in your own inner-guidance system to do what feels right. This is an intuitive process. Relax into it and enjoy the inspirational insights and guidance that come to you seemingly out of the blue.

Moon lover, you've got this!

MOONBEAM INSIGHT
(ONE-CARD PULL)

This is a succinct single-card reading for instant guidance.

- Shuffle the cards.
- Invoke the moon guides for celestial support.
- With devoted intention, ask a question.
- Hold the deck up to the moon to activate with magical moonbeams.
- Knock the deck and imagine mystical moondust infusing the cards.
- Instinctively, select one card from anywhere in the deck.
- Tune in to the card for clear guidance.
- Refer to the guidebook and use your intuition to interpret the meaning.
- Contemplate the card meaning and how it is relevant for you at this time.
- Close the card reading with a heartfelt expression of gratitude.

TRIPLE-MOON INSIGNIA
(THREE-CARD SPREAD)

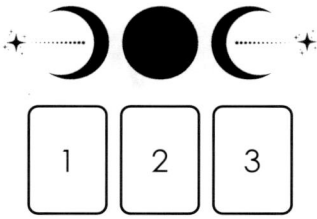

Card One (Left position): Waxing — Growing challenge.

Card Two (Centre position): Full — Complete resolution.

Card Three (Right position): Waning — Inward re-evaluation.

This is a triple-card layout for moving through a challenge and finding a resolution.

- Shuffle the cards.
- Invoke the moon guides for celestial support.
- With devoted intention, focus on the challenge you are currently facing.
- Cup the deck and hold it up to the moon to imbue it with magical moondust.
- Knock the deck and imagine the triple-moon insignia imprinted on the cards.

- Instinctively, select three cards from anywhere in the deck.
- Layout the three cards in a row, from left to right like the diagram.
- Tune in to each of the three cards for clear guidance.
- Refer to the guidebook and use your intuition to interpret the meaning.
- Contemplate the card meanings and how they are relevant to you and the challenge you're experiencing.
- Close the oracle card reading with a heartfelt expression of gratitude.

MOON MAGIC
(THREE-CARD SPREAD)

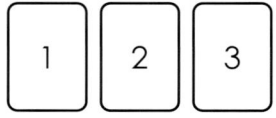

Turn to this three-card layout when calling in your dreamy desires. Create magic with the guidance of the moon and manifest with all your senses and focused intention.

Card One: Summon — Ask for guidance to help you manifest your dreams. This will propel you to the message which is most appropriate for igniting your soul's desires.

Card Two: Wish — Close your eyes and make a wish! Focused intention gives this card more significance and power.

Card Three: Manifest — Explore the magic of manifestation using the ritual and spell chant for this card.

Believe, moon lover! What you have faith in comes true.

- Shuffle the cards.
- Invoke the moon guides for support. They will lead you in the direction of your vision.
- Focus on the desire you are seeking guidance for.
- Prepare for the reading by imagining a white sphere of light encircling you.
- Tap the top of the deck with your knuckles and imagine the cards being infused with an orb of bright white moonlight. This diamond light clarifies and magnifies your intuitive connection.
- Select three cards from anywhere in the deck.
- Place the cards side by side in the order of choosing, as per the diagram.
- Tune in to the card for clear guidance.
- Refer to the guidebook and use your intuition to interpret each card's significance.
- Contemplate the card meanings and how they are relevant to you and what you are currently manifesting.
- Trust, as belief ignites and grants your wishes.

- Close the card reading with a heartfelt expression of gratitude.

LUMINARY
(FIVE-CARD SPREAD)

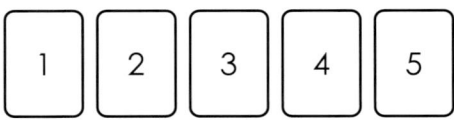

This five-card layout will provide guidance and clarity on your journey forward.

Card One: Birthing phase — Begin.

Card Two: Journey phase — Grow.

Card Three: Impact phase — Hunt.

Card Four: Strength phase — Sustain.

Card Five: Gratitude phase — Celebrate.

- Shuffle the cards with potent and loving intention.
- Invoke the moon guides for celestial support.
- With devoted intention, ask a question or have a clear focus in mind.

- Knock the deck and imagine luminescent light infusing the cards with higher wisdom.
- Instinctively, select five cards from anywhere in the deck.
- Layout the five cards in a row from left to right, as per the diagram.
- Tune in to the cards for clear guidance.
- The five cards provide a pathway to deeper understanding of your current situation.
- Refer to the guidebook and use your intuition to interpret additional insights.
- Contemplate the card meanings and how they are relevant to you.
- Close the card reading with a heartfelt expression of gratitude.

YOUR BIRTH-MOON CARD READING

The phase of the moon you were born under says a lot about you.

You may already know your birth or natal moon, or you may wish to research it online. It's super easy! All you need is your birthdate and an online moon calculator (there are many available on the internet) to decipher what moon you were born under. Different birth moons have unique meanings and traits.

For instance, if you were born on a New Moon, you love new adventures and the honeymoon period of relationships. Waxing-moon souls — you like to progress things, be challenged and continually learn and grow. Full-moon babies — you like to complete things and have a strong sense of achievement. Waning Moon — you are the healers and alchemists, and you love planning for the future.

Get to know yourself better by tuning in to the spiritual qualities and natural inclinations of your natal moon. Harness your lunar-given gifts and learn to navigate your more challenging traits. You may wish to seek direction from the unique lunar guides associated with your birth moon. Enjoy this lunar quest of self-discovery!

- Once you know your birth moon, you can go through the deck and pick out the cards that are linked to your special phase using the Table of Contents at the start of the guidebook.
- Let your intuition guide the number of cards you choose.
- Shuffle the handpicked cards.
- With intention, tune in to the energies of your birth moon and guides for inspiration.
- Tap the top of the deck and imagine the cards lighting up with iridescent moonglow.
- Place cards in a neat pile face down.
- You can decide to either pull cards straight from the top of the pile or fan them out and pull the ones that call to you.

- Refer to the guidebook and use your intuition to interpret each card's significance.
- Dive deeper into each card meaning to seek to know yourself better.
- Intuit the significant signs, symbols, colours, words and images, etc. that pop out.
- Journal on the wisdom that comes through for you, if guided.
- Close your magical practice with gratitude.

TONIGHT'S MOON — PATHWAY READING

Turn to this moon-card reading when seeking immediate guidance by tuning in to the current lunar phase. Keep in mind, although everyone sees the same phases of the moon, the northern and southern hemispheres do see the moon from different angles.

- Discover tonight's moon from a reliable source online.
- Using the Table of Contents at the start of the guidebook, gather the cards that relate to tonight's moon phase.
- Shuffle the cards with grounded intention.
- Invoke the moon guides for higher guidance.
- With sincere intention, focus on the theme you seek spiritual direction for.

- Tap the top of the deck and imagine the cards embossed with tonight's moon phase.
- Place cards in a neat pile, face down.
- You can decide to either pull cards straight from the top of the pile or fan them out and pull the ones that call to your soul.
- Let your intuition guide the number of cards you choose.
- Refer to the guidebook and use your intuition to interpret each card's significance.
- Notice the synchronicities and connections between the cards to map out a clear pathway.
- For further clarity, you may wish to intuitively channel and journal on the accompanying messages.
- Finish your pathway reading with a sincere expression of love, grace and gratitude.

*Follow your own intuitive flow to
dance freely in the moonglow!*

THE NAKED TRUTH AND THE GODDESS

What is the naked truth,
if not the essence of reality?
The unfiltered, unadorned, unmasked expression
of what is
The naked truth is not always pleasant,
nor easy to accept
But it is the only way to see things as they are, and not
as we wish them to be

The goddess is the embodiment of the naked truth, in all
its beauty and power
She does not hide behind illusions,
nor conform to expectations
She is the source of life and the force of nature
She is the creator and the destroyer
She is the lover and the fighter

The goddess invites us to embrace the naked truth and to
live authentically
She challenges us to face our fears,

and grow beyond our limits
She inspires us to love ourselves,
and to love others
She teaches us to honour our bodies
and to honour our spirits

The goddess is the naked truth,
and the naked truth is the goddess
They are one and the same,
and they are within us all
We can access them by listening to our intuition, and by
following our passion
We can manifest them by expressing our creativity, and
by sharing our vision

The naked truth and the goddess are waiting
for us to discover them
Are you ready to meet them?

MUSINGS FROM THE MOON

CARD MEANINGS

ABUK'S MOON TEMPLE: SOUTH SUDAN AND ETHIOPIA

MOON GUIDE

Abuk, also known as Buk or Acol, is the first woman in myths of the Dinka, Muonjang, and Jieng people of South Sudan, the Nile basin and Ethiopia. She is a celebrated female deity of the moon.

PERSONIFICATION

Abuk is the goddess of feminine and moon cycles, water and gardening. She is the guardian of all women and children. She is responsible for the supply of water and ensuring the growth of trees, plants and the productivity of the harvest.

TOTEMS

Abuk's green snake represents fertility, shedding of the old, rebirth, protection, ancestral wisdom, balance and duality. Snakes are revered in South Sudanese culture, believed to be messengers sent by their ancestors. It's considered very unlucky to kill one.

ROOTS

Traditional South Sudanese spirituality centres around a high god called Nhial (also known as Nhialic or Nhialac) as the source of sustenance and a supporting group of deities that embrace Abuk as a chief goddess. Prayers are first addressed to Nhial and then other divinities, clan totems and ancestral spirits are invoked. Today, numerous South Sudanese mix some of their traditional practices with Christianity.

FOLKLORE

One creation story tells of the Creator moulding the first woman, Abuk, and the first man, Garang, out of the rich clay of Sudanese land. It is said that Abuk saved her people from starvation by being resourceful, free-thinking and free-spirited.

MOON-HONOURING TRADITIONS

In South Sudan, ornate ceremonies with lively and colourful rituals, dance and singing are held to celebrate rites of passage, mark significant social gatherings, and for the blessing of people, crops, harvest, cattle, rainfall and, of course, the moon.

1. INSTINCT

I trust my senses to lead me in the direction of my moonlit trail.

MOONLIT CODEWORDS

Protect, Nourish, Nurture

MOONBEAM INSIGHT

It is time to break fresh ground! Find what thrills you and go there. Follow the moon and golden stardust towards infinite horizons. This is your destiny.

A powerful period of rebirth is on the cards for you. Like a snake, you are shedding your skin to reawaken anew.

Circumstances do not make or break you; they simply crack open your heart to learn and grow. A downward spiral is often an inward journey of self-discovery, the perfect time for reflection and an opportunity to change direction.

The love of the lunar mother heals you with nature's green energy of rejuvenation. Refill, revive and then jump back in with renewed enthusiasm! The winds of change blow away dusty cobwebs, so you can rise with the sun and glow like the moon. New pathways will open up and give you a renewed zest for life.

Anytime you have a gut feeling, pay attention and believe in your hunches, as they will never let you down. If you find that sometimes you feel connected and other times you don't, it's just a matter of turning inwards, calming the mind, linking with your heart and reflecting, with the intention to strengthen your spiritual awareness.

MOON GUIDE: ABUK

As the boundless mother of the Dinka, Abuk personifies maternal instinct, ingrained wisdom, resourcefulness and fierce determination. She reawakens and unlocks innate gifts that may be resting dormant, especially psychic and healing abilities.

MOON PHASE: FULL MOON

The Full Moon illuminates the dark and heightens your intuition. It is as if the light of the moon is shining down onto an aspect of yourself that you often keep hidden; a part of yourself that is pure brilliance, but that you keep encased within yourself out of fear that you'll discover your true magnificence.

Break free and shine, moon lover!

FULL MOON RITUAL

With intention, anchor to the earth and breathe softly as you drop into a blissful state. Imagine the moonlight embracing you like a warm mother's hug. Be open to receive any insights that come through. Stay in meditation as long as you feel guided.

INSTINCT SPELL CHANT

Primal mother, comfort and guide me. Even in the darkest of times, I embrace my wild instinct, sharpen my senses and spear of courage, to perceive and hunt down my dreams.

ARTIST PROSE

Sovereign moon of fullness crowned
Stars and spheres of heavens flair
Fierce and roar she stands
Spotted scars of darkened cloaked firm
The peerless coils adorned in kind
Of spiral force of nature's prime
Sustaining knowledge of wisdoms sense
The fierce is you and your ...

2. FREEDOM

I am free to be wholeheartedly me.

MOONLIT CODEWORDS

Break free, Rewild, Sense

MOONBEAM INSIGHT

Unbound personal freedom is on the cards for you.

Right now, you may be the one holding yourself captive. When you break loose from any self-imposed constraints, you have the freedom not just to do what you desire to, but to be who you are destined to be. Your gift of free will and incredible willpower will drive you forward towards a spectacular vision for your life.

Your words and thoughts are vessels of compelling power! Mindfully choose your inner dialogue, as self-awareness is the key to smashing self-inflicted limitations. Be your own best friend, not your own worst enemy.

There may also be a place or situation that does not align with your core values. Have the courage to turn tail and plan your escape. Relinquish any people-pleasing tendencies to break free of the overcompensating patterns that are draining you. Avoiding conflict at all costs to appease others is giving your sovereign authority away. Instead, speak your truth, stand in your divine power and be fiercely protective of your boundaries, so you can soar to the moon effortlessly.

You are an awakened warrior, so operate from a winning stance! Low self-esteem is often the root cause of people-pleasing behaviour. Do you not see how beautiful and brave you truly are? You were born from magical moon and stardust. It's time for a glow up! Self-confidence is the most striking strength you can have. How can anyone see how great you are if you can't see it yourself? When your opinion of yourself grows, then you'll stop trying to get outside validation.

Whatever sets your soul to flight is freedom. Do or die, dearheart! If not now, when? Take a chance, set off on your interstellar quest with trust and enthusiasm. Instinctively sense your way. Be a ball of fire and a self-starter. Stand up and show up!

You may feel compelled to take action, to show initiative and heart-focused leadership to be of service to humanity.

It's time for euphoric liberation!

MOON GUIDE: ABUK

Abuk is the first woman and awakened rebel of the Dinka. Abuk is fierce, brave, wild and free! Abuk can shapeshift into a snake. Her eyes pierce you with intense love. She liberates the soul and refuses to give up on humanity.

MOON PHASE: BALSAMIC MOON

The Waning Crescent or Balsamic Moon is linked to self-devotion. Now is the ideal time to prepare, pivot and get ready to lunge towards your highest vision. Let's break the shackles and slay away everything that may be holding you back from your personal freedom.

BALSAMIC MOON RITUAL

This final phase of the moon is all about reflecting on what came about during this rotation and releasing what is holding you back. Journal on what you want to keep, and what you want to let go of. Were there sabotaging patterns that prevented you from moving towards your wildest dreams? What hidden gems are worth noting? Write it all out in preparation for the next lunar cycle.

FREEDOM SPELL CHANT

Azure smoke of air and cobalt flame of earth, dissolve all harm and fear, only the power of the serpent goddess may enter here. Abuk's tail sweeps away the darkness and captures the moonlight. I free myself from self-inflicted limitations to rise into self-determination.

ARTIST PROSE

The blade of the moon's lucidity severs
Emboldened fearless entwines
Night of heaving shadows sliced of warrior of spirit of heart
Sinews shift on serpentine waves through then and
boundless now

Ferocity pure untamed and true in certainty of self
Freedoms found in treasures birthed of sacred dark and raw
Instinct runs with commanding grace
Offered calls of battles cry
Pure fragrance shed to hearts reborn and re of wilds and you ...

3. SEED

My intentions grow, flourish and thrive.

MOONLIT CODEWORDS

Plan, Cultivate, Ripen

MOONBEAM INSIGHT

Open fully to receive the lavish opulence that is unfurling for you. Your alluring magnetism draws a jam-packed bounty of love to you. The beauty of nature and gifts of the earth are there for the picking. You are the gardener of your life. You get to reap the rewards of all your hard work and dedication.

Seeds represent kernels of wisdom and abundance that inspire generosity, connection, healing and forgiveness. It is time for you to scatter the spiritual seeds of grace and hope across your garden. And, as the New Moon shines, these seeds will grow and gift you luscious fruit and blossoms.

A seed is like an embryo, a precious living thing, but in a sleeping state it must be buried in the sacred earth to activate the growth process. In the darkness, with compassion and understanding, new growth will spring forth. Profound life lessons are germinated in the darkest of days. Never lose hope that the most beautiful flowers bloom from the eternal love of the earth mother. You are loved beyond belief.

Tiny seeds grow, blossom and thrive when nurtured. Ensure you feed and sustain your best-laid plans all the way to completion. Patience is required right now. Be flexible and adapt to different soils and ways of cultivating. Allow the fruit of your labours to ripen naturally on the mother tree. Don't be tempted to pick it too early!

Divine seeds are like valuable lessons. Once planted, observe the insights and lessons that emerge throughout the growth phase. Fragments of enlightenment are everywhere if you open to see the flowers amongst the weeds. Qualities like purity, love, perception and awareness are waiting to fully bloom. Radiate and share your blossoming gifts with the world, moon lover.

MOON GUIDE: ABUK

Abuk, as a mother goddess, is connected with fertility, productivity and the seeding of ideas. Her boundless generosity of spirit glows like the beaming moon in the night sky. Call upon her when bringing new ideas or projects to life.

MOON PHASE: NEW MOON

The beginning of the moon cycle is the perfect time to seed intentions and watch them grow through to the Full Moon. Fertilise your intentions with joy, sprinkle with a little moondust of hope, and nurture your creations with tender loving care.

NEW MOON RITUAL

Buy a packet of flower seeds, a pretty pot and a bag of rich potting mix. Write your wishes on a piece of paper, fold it up and place it at the bottom of the pot. Add soil and sow the seeds. Water regularly, and as your seedlings grow, so do your dreams.

SEED SPELL CHANT

I plant my fertile garden of hope with loving intention. My seeds grow, unfurl and blossom, stretching up to the moon and cascading down to the earth like a petal-suffused waterfall. Flowers dance freely under the moon and the lunar mother smiles.

ARTIST PROSE

Open bright to seed a new existence lush in falls
To swelling moon surge signals breaks
Moist tender fare of richness choice
In lucid earth of cascading life, a-stream
Caressing blooms and butterflies the ripened wings replete
Yearning craves to seasoned needs
Delights of wills that satisfy care potent fruitfulness
Yet want in kind in Sovereign's primal hold
Cherished fields of doublings entwined and ready-full
Yielding you in bliss …

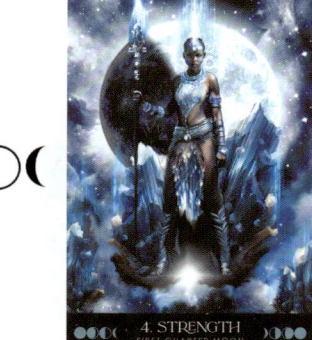

4. STRENGTH

When the going gets tough,
I choose love over fear.

MOONLIT CODEWORDS

Conquer, Foresee, Lead

MOONBEAM INSIGHT

Braveheart, it is time to act and fully commit to your own sacred hunt. Your goals and dreams are yours for the taking, as long as you have the strength and commitment to see the journey through.

The warrior's way is simple: honour your higher purpose to seek soul nourishment. Do not get distracted by outside interference. Stay true to your higher calling. Be fiercely protective of your own energy by strengthening your boundaries.

The secret to harmony is letting every situation be what it is, instead of what you think it should be. Stop trying to control things you have no control over, and instead follow the path of the peaceful warrior. All you can change is yourself, but that often changes everything.

Live in harmony with a peace-loving heart, but also recognise that there are times in life when you will need to stand up and speak up. Your unflinching dedication to what is right—according to your own core values—inspires others. Fighting for something bigger than yourself, demonstrating compassion, leading by example and focusing on service to humanity has its own rewards.

Your fortitude, resourcefulness and inner vision guide you on a winning streak, effortlessly spearing any obstacles that get in your way. Acknowledge your strong points, do not take for granted what you can do and certainly do not settle for anything less than you truly deserve. The warrior spirit does not give up what they love; they find the love in what they do.

Courage, above all things, is the number-one quality of a spirit warrior. Daring to be vulnerable is accepting the emotional risk that comes from being open to love and be loved. Being vulnerable as a leader of light involves a change in attitude that enables you to see through the eyes of the souls you lead. Openness is about meaningful heart-to-heart connection. As you fully show up and are present in the moment, your relationships deepen and are infused with loving intention.

MOON GUIDE: ABUK

Abuk saved humanity from starvation by being resourceful, astute and self-determined. She personifies freedom, free thought, free will and willpower. She declares, "Deep down you know what you want and why you want it. Carry out your plans with a brave heart."

MOON PHASE: FIRST QUARTER MOON

The First Quarter Moon is a time where decisions need to be made and obstacles are overcome. During this phase, half the moon is illuminated and the other half in shadow. Keep a balanced approach to your situation, seek the potential possibilities and pitfalls, and then leap without hesitation.

FIRST QUARTER MOON RITUAL

It is time to set clear objectives and follow through with sheer determination and optimism.

Write down your core focus and then any ideas spiralling out from the centre. Add branches of related thoughts, colours, images and symbols to spur creative thinking. Using this information, map out a way forward and execute your plan with your warrior spirit.

STRENGTH SPELL CHANT

Here and now before the earth and moon goddess, I open my eyes to see what I could not see before. I open my heart to feel what I could not feel before. I open my mind to know what I did not know before. My inner strength, wisdom and undying determination lead the way.

ARTIST PROSE

Spears ahead of keenly edged
Of first of then of now
Foreseen in lead of insights point
Above, below, akin, commitment wisdoms high
To power waves of crystalline

*Of brave and heart and four
In shadow curves in lines of well
Flow state airs within align
Creative care of portents pull
For you forever stands …*

AELUA'S MOON TEMPLE: PORTUGAL

MOON GUIDE
Aelua is the divine embodiment of the moon in ancient Portuguese culture.

In ancient times, Portugal was known as Lusitania in the south, Gallaecia in the north and Al-Andalus on the Iberian Peninsula. Being thousands of years old and from one of the oldest cultures in Europe, Goddess Aelua is one of the first known feminine divinities. Unfortunately, there is little archaeological evidence and sacred texts about her.

PERSONIFICATION
In Portuguese *lua* means 'moon', so as a deity, Aelua personifies the actual moon. She represents water, the infinite expanse of the universe, and the wisdom of age. She withstands the test of time! Many have tried to erase Aelua, but she continues to gleam with everlasting grace. Her hidden mysteries add to her allure.

TOTEMS
Aelua's red roses signify sacred sensuality. Her red shroud veils her hidden mysteries. Her mantilla and crown hint at her role as the sovereign woman, life-bearing vessel and wisdom keeper.

ROOTS

Aelua originates from Lusitanian territory, which is now Guarda in Portugal. She has a diverse and very ancient ancestry, including Iberian, pre-Celtic, Moor, Roman and German, just to name a few. Temple ruins, mosques and churches are layered one upon the other throughout Portugal due to its rich cultural history. Today, the main religion of Portugal is Roman Catholic, although ancient traditions are still woven within.

FOLKLORE

When the Romans conquered Portugal, Portuguese myths mixed with Roman beliefs, so it is possible that the Roman goddess Luna is a descendant of the eternal Aelua. She is sister to the sun goddess, Asidia and the earth goddess, Ilurbeda.

MOON-HONOURING TRADITIONS

Chamarrita is a Portuguese festival where women wear goddess crowns, dresses and flowers as part of New and Full Moon ceremonies. This ancient festival of feeding the entire town for free is still celebrated today in Portugal and Portuguese-speaking countries, like Brazil. Traditional folk dances, street parades and feasts celebrate the moon goddess.

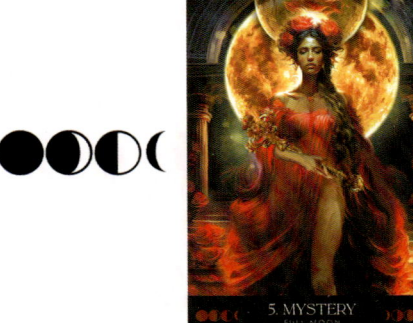

5. MYSTERY

I embody my unique, captivating charm.

MOONLIT CODEWORDS

Allure, Discover, Unveil

MOONBEAM INSIGHT

Open to the mystery of magic!

The 'seen and the unseen' wonders of creation are opening for you. You'll be surprised and delighted by the curiosities that will sprinkle your path with magical moondust and bring unexpected opportunities your way.

Mystery is all around you, touching you in the deepest parts of yourself. You are being called to be a wayshower. Observe the spiritual hints and clues by being fully present and awake to the synchronicities. Be curious and inquisitive. Divine the hidden truth. Learn to harness the magical moments and consciously create your very own enchanting wonderland.

Devotion to spiritual service brings soul enlightenment and deeper meaning to your life. Your dedication to an honourable cause lifts your spirit and the vibration of the planet. Never underestimate your impact on the world around you.

Immersed in light and shrouded in mystery, your spiritual radiance and natural magnetism creates ripples of desirability and draws miracles to you. You are captivating!

Embrace your true nature and authentic essence by shedding the masks, roles and obligations that no longer align to your current truth. Like attracts like, love attracts love. Follow your heart's desires, interests and creative gifts to cultivate genuine happiness. Happy people are way more magnetic than people forcing themselves through life. Doing even a bit more of what you love every day can help you feel more intimately connected to life. Bring into line everything that matches your divine potential and watch the magic happen.

MOON GUIDE: AELUA

Goddess Aelua reminds you that your divine connection and sacred roots are born from the mother of creation. Through spiritual unity with Aelua, you enter the heart portal within yourself where you can activate, initiate and reawaken your connection to moon magic.

MOON PHASE: FULL MOON

Full Moon activations unearth elemental magic. The ebb and flow of the ocean, earth and lunar energies dance in unison to attract blessings to you. When you allow these elements to weave together, you will be blown away by the serendipity that will show up in your everyday life.

FULL MOON RITUAL

Connect with moon and ocean magic to cast a magical spell upon your life. You do not need to be near the sea to harness her mystery. Imagine the moon kissing the ocean with her luminous light and then with strong loving intention recite the mystery spell chant below.

MYSTERY SPELL CHANT

I walk my sacred path, embracing my inborn magic, a place where I am alive with the mystery of the moon. Waves of moonlight wash away anything that conceals my oneness with the Divine. In mystical ecstasy, the illusion of separation softens and dissolves. I emerge renewed!

ARTIST PROSE

Sacred waves bewitched in stillness pierced
Of breath and sigh and rose
Unfurled of spirits roiled in gold
Molten blooms through rivers run
In heated shades of temptress charmed
Enthralled in hallowed awe
Whispered hush unknown is draped encircled sheer of flame
Temples inspired full enlivened light, loved passion deep profound
Fervent pressed desires of self
In halo's moon the mysteries lay for you …

6. Patience

I personify serenity.

MOONLIT CODEWORDS

Wait, Entice, Catch

MOONBEAM INSIGHT

Your persistence is being rewarded. Your dreams are in the making! Have faith!

Brilliant imaginings will come to life at the right time for you. Positivity is like a magnet. Keep a hopeful attitude while you wait and stay calm no matter what happens. Know with optimism and fortitude that everything is possible.

Where your focus goes, energy flows! And where energy flows, whatever you're focusing on grows. Meaning that your life is strongly influenced by what you concentrate on and give your time and energy to. That's why you must focus on where you want to go, not on what you fear.

Patience is a powerful attractor; it allows things to unfold naturally. When you force, push and doubt your dreams, you are repelling the natural flow of the universe. Synchronise to the pace of nature and everything will happen in divine harmony.

The power of surrender is the secret key to manifesting success in all areas of life — including your work, relationships and wellbeing. Surrender dissolves doubt and the fatigue that comes from 'trying too hard'. It supports you to achieve goals more easily and brings ongoing inner peace. You will enjoy life's journey much more when you stop to smell the roses.

There is a well-known saying: "Good things come to those who wait." Patience allows you to progress with ease and grace, and helps you make more aligned decisions that often lead to even greater accomplishments. Patient people have a better sense of gratitude. Not only is having genuine appreciation a beautiful way to see and experience the world, living in an attitude of gratitude also magnetises exciting prospects to you more effortlessly.

It is important to recognise that setbacks are really opportunities in disguise. Things may not be clear right now but have heart and do not give up. Persist and see where you are guided to go. Trust the process and know that your dreams are coming to fruition. Flow forward in faith and everything else will take care of itself.

MOON GUIDE: AELUA

Goddess Aelua declares: *"Nothing is lacking, everything will come to you in the exact right moment. Patience is a strength and you, dearheart, are strong. Commit to your soul's purpose regardless of how long it takes. Trust the divine timing of your sacred quest. Enjoy the unfoldment."*

MOON PHASE: NEW MOON

The New Moon reminds you that your dreams and your life are all worthy of your persistence, love and trust. Plant seeds of hope right now and witness the growth through to the Full

Moon phase with inquisitive delight and heartfelt gratitude.

NEW MOON RITUAL

First, choose a crystal and begin by thanking it for its service. Ask your crystal to transmute that which holds you back from living freely. Give everything to the gem that you want to release and alchemise. Cleanse your crystal in the New Moonlight, under running water or by burying it in the earth.

PATIENCE SPELL CHANT

My impatience must come to an end. Serenity is my goddess-given strength. I will be patient and this, I do declare. I surrender to my higher being. I let go and let love in. I set myself free. I trust in the unknown. Healing is in my hands. I am blessed.

ARTIST PROSE

Advent moon and guide of ways
Times of witness divine in faith
Yearning hearts as distance calls in serenades song
Salted mists of resonate waves in lights bright lines
Resound in silence but for the wind of eternity

Compendium foretells the coming of hope
Wilds held dear and courage faced in blooms of pure nights glow
Awaiting of soul
Of forever and now
Feeling your way to you ...

7. GRATITUDE

I am eternally thankful.

MOONLIT CODEWORDS

MAGNIFY, PEAK, RELEASE

MOONBEAM INSIGHT

You can breathe a long-awaited sigh of relief. The bursting Full Moon overflows with an ocean of promise. Aelua the glowing goddess of gratitude smiles on you. Good fortune is mounting. Have faith that any current money worries will wane.

The glow of the moonlight illuminates the endless opportunities opening up for you, as well as a greater awareness of your life's purpose. When you follow your higher calling, a steady stream of prosperity is a natural consequence. Don't be afraid to listen to your heart.

Appreciating your blessings is the root of all abundance. Gratitude is one of the most productive emotions. It's about deliberately focusing on what is good, being thankful for the things you already have and pausing to appreciate the things that often get taken for granted. It means learning to live your life as if everything is a miracle and being aware of how much you have been gifted. You will be astounded by the magic that can happen when you have spiritually aware eyes in which to see it.

The moon has no light of her own, so when she is shining at her brightest, we are receiving crowning glory from the sun's rays bouncing off her surface. At the time of the Full Moon, the lunar energies are at their strongest. These escalating energies have the power to amplify, so be mindful of your inner and outer dialogue at this time. Ensure your communication remains upbeat and gracious.

MOON GUIDE: AELUA

Goddess Aelua bridges the celestial and physical realms. She creates Heaven on Earth. As an embodiment of the Full Moon, Aelua expands and cultivates a reassuring feeling of appreciation, clear psychic awareness and perception.

MOON PHASE: FULL MOON

If you were climbing a mountain, the Full Moon signifies the peak. Although it is not the completion of the journey, it is a significant pause point, a time to step back and reflect on how far you have come and to appreciate where you are.

FULL MOON RITUAL

A ritual at its roots is a practice of embodiment, it takes things from the intangible and makes them tangible. A divine way to do this is by writing a gratitude list. On the next Full Moon, journal what you are celebrating with these lush lunar energies and get into the feeling of gratitude.

GRATITUDE SPELL CHANT

By the powers of the Full Moon and Goddess Aelua, I bless this gratitude journal. I attract luck by aligning to an attitude of gratitude. My soul is forever grateful. This is my will, so mote it be.

ARTIST PROSE

Fullness leads her genius bright
In lustres gleam inspiring ways
Heavenly rounds of labyrinths sway
Moonlight crowned lunation full
Of starlight-ness bejewelled
Diffusion surged through beauties light
Of gracious heart and brimming worth
Nobility vast in cosmic charms
Enhanced to crest the surety strides
Prospects of you made real ...

8. PROTECTION

*I remove all my masks to unveil
the face of my soul.*

MOONLIT CODEWORDS

Preserve, Shield, Save

MOONBEAM INSIGHT

Open your wings of light to soar upwards! You are ready to ascend into higher dimensions. Now is the time to remain committed to your core values, highest priorities and soul purpose. Your unwavering faith, self-reliance and ability to rise above any dread and doubt ensures your success and ultimate victory.

Safeguard yourself from negativity that drags you down, protect your boundaries and practise healthy detachment to sustain your peak vibration, performance and energy levels. Once you establish your boundaries, you can bare your soul and be vulnerable knowing you are completely protected and safe. Learn to say 'no' to situations that deplete you and 'yes' to circumstances that lift you up.

On guard! Your sword of light creates a shield of love that is impenetrable. You are being called to soften and release unnecessary worry to reveal the depths of your inner beauty. Your soul beauty goes beyond your personality, physical body and life story. It's rooted in divine love. Come up out of the darkness of worthlessness, take off your mask and be your authentic self!

As an instinctive person you have the natural ability to camouflage yourself, adapt to your environment and communicate intuitively. Like the chameleon, you have the gift to blend in, change at will and be flexible. The symbolic representation of camouflage is sacred freedom, power and purpose. This agility and transformative power are hidden talents. Embrace your gifts!

MOON GUIDE: AELUA

Lunar goddess, Aelua, is known as the winged warrior, truth seeker and protectress of divine love. She transmutes fear into love, doubt into certainty and misunderstanding into clarity. Her sword of light illuminates the hidden beauty in the world and the universal truth of Oneness unity.

MOON PHASE: GIBBOUS MOON

The gibbous moon offers increased awareness around your personal space and safety. It's a time to fortify your boundaries and retreat within your physical temple to recharge the batteries and realign to your heart centre.

GIBBOUS MOON RITUAL

Protection magic transforms negative energy into positive. Jewellery is a terrific way to harness this magic in your daily life. Try wearing protective crystals like black obsidian, tourmaline or smoky quartz. Find gems that call out to you and make you feel powerfully protected.

PROTECTION SPELL CHANT

I impart only love. I know that when love is in my heart, fear cannot exist. This alchemy transforms all unwanted energies into the lunar light of Goddess Aelua. I allow my life to flow with grace. I seek beauty and align to the sacred code of divine love. I am safe. Amen.

ARTIST PROSE

Mettle donned in wings of grace
Realms masked foreseen and un
Suppressions guise shields the guarded round
Compassed sphere of cambered dark in range
Celestial thoughts diverged from space
In worlds of scores of lucent gentle eases
Soothing steel forged keenly bright
Autonomous in light held palmed
Couraged souls sky-clad in faith
Danced fair in edges held
Hammers ring valours grit for you ...

CERRIDWEN'S MOON TEMPLE: CELTIC

MOON GUIDE

Cerridwen is the main Celtic lunar goddess. As goddess of the Underworld and keeper of the cauldron of knowledge, she is often referred to as the dark-moon goddess or crone mother of inspiration and rebirth. In addition to the moon, Cerridwen is associated with herbal remedies, fertility matters, feminine cycles, science, psychic arts and poetry.

PERSONIFICATION

Cerridwen is a Welsh sorceress and white witch. She embodies poetic wisdom, inspiration and prophecy. As a white witch, she uses her gifts and cauldron to help others. She is also a shapeshifter, meaning she can transform into any age, as well as any animal, like the sow, hound, otter, hawk and hen.

TOTEMS

Her totems include the cauldron, oak tree, lakes and, of course, the moon. Her cauldron is symbolic of the womb as a feminine vessel, the oak tree represents her wisdom while lakes signify her as the giver of fertility. Cerridwen's moon represents the unending cycle of rebirth.

ROOTS

Although she is likely much older, references to Cerridwen as an enchantress can be found in Welsh medieval poetry dating back to the 12th century. Cerridwen may also be connected with the ancient Druids of the first century BCE who are sometimes referred to as 'Knowers of the Oak Tree'. Today, Cerridwen is celebrated as a pagan and Wiccan goddess. Wicca is a modern-day, nature-based religion. Cerridwen's sacred site is the beautiful Bala Lake in North Wales.

FOLKLORE

It is said that Cerridwen brewed a potion for her son, Morfran, to grant him beauty and wisdom. Her subsequent tales explore the lessons around growth through transformation, not fearing change, anything being possible and finding the answers you seek within.

MOON-HONOURING TRADITIONS

Cerridwen was celebrated through poetry, prayer and song. Offerings were made in her honour by setting up an altar with a cauldron and lighting a white candle under the moon.

9. FATE

I interlace my destiny with the gift of free will.

MOONLIT CODEWORDS

Weave, Connect, Be aware

MOONBEAM INSIGHT

Goddess Cerridwen's web of life speaks of all pathways being interconnected. Her totem, the spider, represents the infinite possibilities the web of magic holds for you. Be reassured that you are on the right path.

The wise woman inspires you to take control of your own fate. Sometimes we are on the threshold of bursting into a thousand stars, but we procrastinate and postpone our very own supernova. We decide, "Maybe tomorrow." Cerridwen implores you not to wait! Take advantage of the momentum and divine timing in this moment. She heartens you to consciously create your own luck. You have the power!

You are being called back to nature. Walk through a forest, connect with the trees and feel your heart connection to the sacred earth through the soles of your feet and your soul's core. Getting back to nature in this way will help you find your north star and connect with your own personal mission statement.

Embrace your own unique qualities and harness your natural rhythm, intuitive flow and the mystical moon cycles to plan and implement your creative ideas. Stay true to you, regardless of what is happening around you. Focus only on what you can control. Fate will take care of the rest.

MOON GUIDE: CERRIDWEN

The Welsh goddess Cerridwen has many titles and facets: White Lady of Fate, Weaver of Time, Great Queen and Wise Crone, to name a few. She is both fate and death, the cradle and the grave. She is also a powerful protectress, sage witch and healer.

MOON PHASE: WAXING CRESCENT MOON

Out of the darkness comes the Waxing Crescent Moon, lighting the way forward to new galaxies and exhilarating adventures. This growing luminary sees the sun moving closer to the moon and beginning to illuminate it. This phase is the time to deliberately set intentions.

WAXING CRESCENT MOON RITUAL

Take inspired action using this deck. Breathe, focus on your wishes, shuffle the cards and spread out in a crescent shape. Hover your hands over the cards until you feel a pull and draw two cards: the first brings clarity and the second pinpoints the action needed.

FATE SPELL CHANT

I am the cauldron in which all ingredients blend together in Oneness unity. I am the web of creation that weaves prevailing magic. I am the healer of deep wounds, the wise witch who rights all wrongs. I am divine justice tempered with clemency.

ARTIST PROSE

Silver threads they weave
Cosmic time of stardust's frost
In winters web weft it drums
To ancients One of conscious ken
Blueprints formed in magics shared
Genius sparked in snowflakes whorl
The watching gaze of patterns light
They flitter along the starlight paths
Your footfalls dance in fractal perfection ...

10. INNOCENCE

I am the flower child of pure love.

MOONLIT CODEWORDS

Unfurl, Emerge, Bloom

MOONBEAM INSIGHT

Embrace your childlike virtue! Your open, trusting nature unleashes unbridled creativity and untamed imagination. Wide-eyed in wonder and unaffected by outside influences, your potential is limitless. Hold onto this wildness and remain curious and spontaneous.

When you're pure of heart, magical doors spring open. A full life is a collection of tiny miracles. Cherish the little moments that spring seemingly from nowhere. Make the most of these bright buds of joy and laugh often. Effervescent giggles lighten your burdens and liberate your spirit.

Simple abundance is seeking beauty in nature and modest everyday rituals. Notice the tweeting birds, buzzing bees and moonlight peeping through the blossoming branches. Be on the lookout for the wise baby owl, sharing her whispers of wisdom in the shadows of the trees. She speaks of doing those things that make you truly happy! Be open to exploring the myriad of ways that joy can flutter into your patch of paradise.

The flower-faced baby owl gently guides you to sidestep the potholes on the trail and not be bothered by the bumps in the night that threaten to throw you off course. It doesn't matter how many frights and yowls happen in the moonlit night, the humble and small are always there to offer their astute guidance and delicious delights. Sense your way gracefully to a bright new day.

MOON GUIDE: BLODEUWEDD

Blodeuwedd means *flower-faced*. As the maiden of spring, she holds the promise of warmth and new life after the cold and bareness of Cerridwen's winter.

MOON PHASE: NEW MOON

Your New Moon journey is one of resurgence. Be brave, little one! You are unfurling your wings of light and petals of hope. You are reawakening your true self. Just like the New Moon, your greatest gifts will come in times of darkness.

NEW MOON RITUAL

The New Moon is a divine time to declutter your home, your head and your heart. It is surprising what will grow in freshly cultivated earth. Decluttering your home and office on a New Moon makes space for abundant growth.

INNOCENCE SPELL CHANT

Pure of heart, I whisper to trees, laugh with flowers, fall in love with the moon, dance with the stars and fly free with the butterflies. I clear my path with sparkling intention. Today I choose to be happy. So may it be.

ARTIST PROSE

Lucid hush of sable moon in dark
Of blossomed air sweet-scented wings
Shifting buds and adoring eyes, bright from the light within
Wide with wisdoms passed through gentled brush
Joys of feathered and purest touch
Of virtues clarity unsullied
Unfurl from burdens of heavy minds
And listen for the silent flight
Upon wings of wonder
Nature's call to curious of spirit ... to you.

11. PROWESS

I embrace what is and accept what comes.

MOONLIT CODEWORDS

Trust, Discern, Decide

MOONBEAM INSIGHT

Maeve, the queen of the fae, blazes her light of sovereign wisdom and loving reassurance. She declares, "Your time is now!"

Your hunger for more passion and meaning in your life has led you here. Magical momentum is building. All your preparation and practice are paying off. The time, effort and energy you've put in is bringing great progress. Decisive action in the direction of your goals aligns you to call in more opportunities and challenges that seed growth.

Be daring! When you feel fear, trust and leap with conviction anyway. Calculated risks will pay off! When you let go and trust, you create more space for what ignites your fire. Follow your intuition to flame your new desires.

You have honed your skills and become so proficient in your chosen field, it is now time to relax, enjoy and reap the rewards. There is no longer any need to overcompensate. Open all your senses to fully experience and enjoy the pleasures of what you are consciously creating.

Your bravery, determination and skillset underpin your success. Don't dim your own radiant light. You're only just getting started. Don't pull the pin too early, turn up the heat instead!

Rule over your own domain, intoxicating one! You are a magnetic force of creation.

MOON GUIDE: MAEVE

Maeve is known by many different titles: Mother, Faery Queen, Medb of the Sidhe, Intoxicating One and She Who Rules. Her body is the lifeblood and creative force of the earth, sacred fire, rushing waters, running horses, majestic mountains and fertile fields.

MOON PHASE: FULL MOON

This is the time to surrender and make space for fresh energy to support your intentions. Maeve dances ecstatically with the moon cycles and is in full swing at the Full Moon. Her wish is that you surrender all perceived restraints to flow freely into the sacred flames of desire.

FULL MOON RITUAL

Maeve's full-moon embodiment practice requires free-spirited, fearless, uninhibited and elated dancing. Actively seek the sacred in the interconnectedness of everything through this divinely inspired dance ritual. Envision Maeve's spark of creation twirling around you like fire in a magical spiral of light.

PROWESS SPELL CHANT

My protector and moon guide, Maeve, queen of the faeries, I call you to my side. With your fire spark flowing through my veins, I declare with real intent: I am the magic! I have brilliant prowess within me. I am fearless, free and self-determining. So may it be.

ARTIST PROSE

Antlers king in queening crown
Forests zeal untamed
Eager's blaze passed through heated lips of thirst and hungered brave
Inspired flowers and auburn wilds the lust it Fae's in call
Unkempt it thrills temptations vital certain storm
Aroused and roused her siren's spark ignites
With ventures dared in natures heard enlivened in beauty's bright
Through doyens' cry of whispers charms intoxicates desire
The sovereign she and magics born
Sing to you, your valiant fire …

12. REBIRTH

Let me be born again.

MOONLIT CODEWORDS

Wish, Transform, Merge

MOONBEAM INSIGHT

Goddess Cerridwen's cauldron of poetic inspiration and conscious creation is brewing up your brilliant manifestations as we speak. Your heart's desires are coming together effortlessly for you. Trust!

Transformation requires acceptance of your current situation and full awareness of what you need to implement to create a positive change in your life. Cerridwen's spirit stirs your creative juices, motivates and instils you with the confidence you need to act on your dreams. She activates your soul memory, so your hidden gifts can bubble to the surface.

Cerridwen declares, "You don't need to change, you just need to recall your sacred power!"

You are being called to fully embody your spirituality for your own personal growth. Come back into your divine body and open up to deeply feel through all your senses, including the intuitive ones. Become aware of who you truly are, what your patterns are and what you communicate without words. Develop a healthy relationship with yourself, others and the wider realm.

It's time to get out of your mind and into a heart space of giving and receiving with grace. Live in and from your wholeness. Truly inhabit every single cell of your powerful body. Every organ carries a message. Every beat of your heart asks you to use that power wisely. Remember and honour your body's power to heal and regenerate itself every day. In the same way, you have the power within to be born again.

MOON GUIDE: CERRIDWEN

Cerridwen comes from the Welsh word *cerd* meaning 'poetry' or 'song' and *wen* meaning 'white', 'fair' or 'holy'. Goddess Cerridwen is the keeper of the cauldron and represents knowledge, inspiration and alchemy. She rules the realms of cycles, fertility, regeneration, enchantment and knowledge.

MOON PHASE: DARK MOON

Mysterious moonless nights are viewed as a time of inward reflection, quiet contemplation and intention setting. If the New Moon plants seeds of inspiration, the Dark Moon fertilises those intentions. The Dark Moon is the Waning Crescent Moon right before the New Moon.

DARK MOON RITUAL

Create sacred space in honour of Goddess Cerridwen. Place a cauldron on your altar symbolising the cosmic womb of creation. Beautify your altar with candles, apples, grains, acorns, honeysuckle, branches and crystals for fertility. Meditate on making positive changes and visualise it coming to fruition.

REBIRTH SPELL CHANT

I call on Cerridwen and her cauldron of creation. We stir, blend and merge our magic. I harness the sacred power of transformation and magical divination. I am reborn again, and again, and again. My soul is eternal.

ARTIST PROSE

Green of wise and sacred earth
In veins and vines abound
Silken scent drifts pure of Lunas dulcet charms
Unfurled arms leafed trinkets lay of flowered enthrals of rite
On bitter bound through cauldron's coiled yon silver of the stars
Yet not of worn or thinning veils enheartened power reigns
Called forth and through, beyond and in, kept dear to honoured bid
Awaited paths of covenants roots entwined and gathered cloak
Freedoms sweep of wing-ed-night turns to alchemy's dawn
In ringing songs and sounding bells for you she is nature's borne …

DIANA'S MOON TEMPLE: ROME

MOON GUIDE
Diana is the Roman goddess of the hunt, wild animals and lunar magic. Similar to her Greek counterpart Artemis, she is wild, free and brave. Women who wished to conceive a baby would pray to Diana and those escaping domestic violence, slavery or coercion would seek her protection and guidance.

PERSONIFICATION
Diana embodies characteristics of the sacred quest, hunt, fertility, self-reliance and authenticity. She is seen as a fearless guardian of women, children, and the vulnerable or marginalised. She personifies courage, determination, independence and sacred rebellious qualities.

TOTEMS
Diana's main symbol is the Crescent Moon that hovers behind her in the starry night sky. Her other symbols include the bow and quiver, deer and hunting dogs that represent her self-determination, instinctual guidance and courage to move forward fearlessly.

ROOTS

Diana is an early Greco-Roman goddess. Offering refuge and protection to all, the Temple of Diana was built in the sixth century BCE in ancient Rome. Another temple in her honour, named 'Diana's Mirror', is a natural sanctuary near the sacred grove of Aricia at Lake Nemi in the Lazio Region of Italy, located south of Rome.

FOLKLORE

Originally, Roman deities were thought to be divine presence and without physical form. By the third century BCE, Diana is chronicled to be among the 12 main divinities of the Greco-Roman pantheon. One myth centres around Diana bathing in the woods and turning a predatory hunter into a deer that is torn apart by his own dogs.

MOON-HONOURING TRADITIONS

The Nemoralia was a three-day festival held in honour of Goddess Diana where her devotees would light candles and torches, wear garlands and wreaths, and offer prayers and gifts to Diana by tying ribbons and leaving amulets near water. It is thought that the Catholic Church may have adapted the Nemoralia festival as the Feast of Assumption.

13. HUNT

Everything I seek is within me.

MOONLIT CODEWORDS

Aim, Launch, Surrender

MOONBEAM INSIGHT

Your spiritual direction is being driven by your higher purpose, motives and priorities. Action with conscious intention fuels your journey and ensures a positive outcome. Be on the lookout for meaningful signs, symbols and synchronicities that point you in the direction of your wildest dreams. Seek the petals of wisdom and bright inspiration that spring forth like dancing wildflowers on the forest trail.

Feel the power of Diana, goddess of the hunt, run through your veins and seed the flower of wisdom in your heart. You may be questioning out-of-date beliefs, assumptions and meanings in your realm at present. Growing pains bring positive shifts, evolutionary growth and transformation. Like a snake, be slinky, flexible and adaptable to gently shed your old skin to be reborn afresh. Stay the course and you will be rewarded.

Master the direction of your attention, braveheart. Surrender to a state of allowing, of total openness within, and release the need to forcefully control everything. As you surrender, you will receive the steps and divine guidance you need. When you let go of the resistance and instead focus on your desires, you will flow forward in full faith.

Remember, the moment you desire something, it plants a seed that grows into a blossoming bud. Trust the process. Deepen your connection to source energy by vibrating on the frequency of love, grace and gratitude. Match your thoughts, feelings and actions to the energy of Source. Live in the now! Remember everything is happening right now — the past and future are all illusions of the mind. Your success is already guaranteed.

MOON GUIDE: DIANA

Goddess Diana represents the seer, truth seeker and huntress archetypes. She is the goddess of the wildwoods, moon and sacred quest. Her name is derived from the Latin word *dium* meaning 'sky' and *dius* meaning 'light'. She shines her moonbeams afar, so you can see the bigger picture.

MOON PHASE: GIBBOUS MOON

The Waxing Gibbous Moon, also known as the expansion lunar phase, is the most aligned time for you to shine your whole light and focus on trusting your own magic. The Waning Gibbous Moon, when the moon is decreasing, is the idyllic time to take a breather and make space for new beginnings.

GIBBOUS MOON RITUAL

Place your hand on your heart, find your own heartbeat and then attune to the universal heartbeat. Softly close your eyes and go within, focus on the ebb and flow of the sacred breath. On the out breath, give yourself permission to fully let go and surrender. Continue to breathe. All is well.

HUNT SPELL CHANT

I am the seer, truth seeker and huntress. I am at home in the forest. I embrace my true nature. I rewild to be free and wholeheartedly me. I harness my inborn wisdom and goddess-given gifts.

ARTIST PROSE

Nature of three seeds to one transformed
Sky moon silent she pulls
Raw power dear to heart
Through trees of cosmic heeds
Steadfast point
Spirit's scent unbound
The press of earth in rainbowed hues
Shifts bend of twig afoot
Sky-clad sight peers through the haze
Plunge deep in wilding-self...

14. FERTILITY

I celebrate new beginnings with bubbly anticipation.

MOONLIT CODEWORDS

Conceive, Perceive, Believe

MOONBEAM INSIGHT

Wild moon child, it's time to start something new and trust in the miracle of creation. Magnificent new beginnings, a fresh start and clean slate are on the cards for you.

Plant the seeds of something new and cultivate your seedlings with tender loving care. Take delight in the sprouting growth. There is no need to rush. You will reap the rewards of your attentive planning and preparation. Moondust to soil — this planting stage will flourish and flower for you.

Always keep your head up, as you never know what awaits you. Remember, what you seek is seeking you. Don't shy away from new networks and surroundings that inspire you. Observe the unexpected ways and surprising places that are blooming for you right now. Be open to new and improved methods of doing things, embrace new chances at happiness and consider the boundless options opening up at the beginning of this new phase.

The only way is up from here. Don't look back, stay grounded in the present moment and get excited about your foreseeable future. Despite any personal challenges, you will grow stronger, wiser and more resourceful.

Optimism opens you up to higher dimensions. Confidence grows self-assurance. What you believe, you receive. So, faith it until you make it. Unfurl your petals and open fully to accept the bouquet of budding possibilities. Move forward gracefully with your head held high and dance in joyful flow.

It's time for you to turn the page, an exciting chapter is just beginning. Don't forget to enjoy the journey as you go and have fun exploring this novel adventure.

MOON GUIDE: DIANA

Goddess Diana is a dedicated guardian of children and protector of childbirth. She also supports fertility, growth and motherhood. Diana sprinkles her moondust like seeds of hope. She brings new opportunities and offers fertile soil for your intentions.

MOON PHASE: NEW MOON

The New Moon is the dream seed time! It is a more reflective time in the lunar cycle and signifies new life as we plant seeds in the lush earth for future growth. It's the divine time for self-analysis, meditation and intention setting.

NEW MOON RITUAL

Under the light of the New Moon, invoke Goddess Diana for her loving support and lunar magic. Light a candle, get into a blissful relaxed state and take some time to reflect on your desires. When you are ready, write down your intentions as a wish list.

FERTILITY SPELL CHANT

On the New Moon night, I shall weave my magic for all the blessings I want to receive. In my heart, I will believe. Dear Goddess Diana, warrior of the Divine. If you have heard my call, show me a sign.

ARTIST PROSE

Silvered light of night moon's song
Nourishment borne in tempered bliss
Divinity once more
Nurtured spark shimmers to flower
With Goddess moon in lightless held
Embers quickened in star-filled wombs
Boundless souls of night skies
Belief the hands of Goddess held
You — lush with blossom promise ...

15. TRUTH

My reality is ever evolving.

MOONLIT CODEWORDS

Consider, Reveal, Cultivate

MOONBEAM INSIGHT

You may be questioning your views at present and experiencing a huge paradigm shift in how you see the world. These growing pains are activating intense spiritual growth for you.

You are on the edge of the mystery and purpose of your life. Embrace it. Embody the curiosity and inquisitiveness of your inner moon child. We never stop learning, growing and evolving. Allow the truth to reveal itself to you. An open mind and heart create graceful flow and flexibility to help you see the bigger picture.

Seasons, cycles and outside influences all affect your perception of your current situation. In other words, your lived experience affects the lens you see through. See past the obvious to dig deeper and seek the truth of the matter at hand.

Move through every breath with real courage to be guided home to your spirit. Stay true to your own divinity, core values and purpose, regardless of the pressure you may be under to act otherwise. Align your values, ideals and actions to live a congruent and harmonious existence.

Be honest with yourself and with others and take responsibility for your slip-ups. Remember, healing is in your hands. Whatever you have said or done before, accept it, grow from it and forgive yourself. Stop hiding from the shadows of the past. Do not be trapped in the darkness of shame and shattered dreams. Let the light of love permeate your being and shine upon you. Immerse yourself in an ocean of compassion to set your soul free. Forgive yourself because it is the only way to start afresh.

MOON GUIDE: DIANA

Diana is the twin sister of Sun God Apollo. Her sacred symbol, a Crescent Moon, crowns her in the sky. One of her celestial archetypes is the truth seeker. In unison with the sun, she hunts for clarity and the deeper meaning in life, love and your soul's purpose.

MOON PHASE: THIRD QUARTER MOON

The Third Quarter Moon rises around midnight and sets around noon. At this time, the moon is nearly back to the point in its trajectory where its dayside directly faces the sun and all that you see from our earthly outlook is a small bow. This moon guides you to see the light of your truth and a higher perspective.

THIRD QUARTER MOON RITUAL

Using your journal, reflect on the question, "What lies am I telling myself?" These may be a repetitive story you're stuck in, negative self-beliefs, justification of sabotaging patterns or an outright lie. Be honest with yourself so you can shine a light on your unconscious shadows but remember to be kind and gentle with yourself in the process.

TRUTH SPELL CHANT

Darling Diana, help me to see the hidden truth. Lying to myself is self-defeating. The highest truth is love. I love myself. I trust myself. I forgive myself. I back myself. It is done in divine love.

ARTIST PROSE

The exquisite sting of currents roused untainted full and fierce
From fathoms dark abyss they dwell in flux of candour's hush
'Neath pure of bliss enraptured finds deceit unfiltered true
Abiding eyes of dreaming sprite reveals from instinct's breath
By waters clear of sense and known
Sincerity of ageless deemed
Of heart, of mind, of thoughts, of felts
In verity and states of stream
Of cherished pools, of sacred souls considered and direct
Ocean's feel for your reveal from immortal sounds of depth ...

16. CROSSROAD

All paths lead to love.

MOONLIT CODEWORDS

Contemplate, Choose, Expect

MOONBEAM INSIGHT

Hecate, Queen of the Crossroads, has emerged from the misty shadows because you have arrived at a critical juncture and must make some important decisions. You need to choose a direction and she is the right goddess for the job! Ask Hecate, the wayshower, to lead and light your way.

Take a breath, weigh up the facts, gather all relevant information and consider all consequences before making a decision and choosing your path forward. Hecate speaks of these deciding moments as significant turning points. See beyond the smoke and mirrors to discern the naked truth. Once you've made the call, go your own way with out-and-out confidence knowing that you have practised good judgement.

Allow Hecate's violet flame of transformation to change your indecisiveness into unfaltering faith and self-assurance. Trust her hounds to hunt down the best way forward and protect you from any ambushes and potholes along the trail.

Release any self-doubt embedded in your unconscious mind and shadowy Underworld that may be holding you back. Feel the fear and do it anyway! Alchemise trepidation with your goddess-given gifts of vulnerability and courage.

Exhilarating adventures are unfolding before you. Embrace the dark and mysterious! Soar into the mystical cosmos! Dance and weave under the enchanting moon shadow! These new explorations will expand your mind and open your heart to an endless stream of divine wisdom and love. Be bold and bright, dearheart! Do not be afraid to shine your light.

MOON GUIDE: HECATE

As the goddess of witches, the shadow queen and wayshower, Hecate presides over crossroads and magic. Her powerful influence spread all over ancient Europe and pillars named 'Hecate' stood proudly at crossroads and gateways to protect and light the way.

MOON PHASE: TRIPLE GODDESS MOON — THIRD QUARTER MOON

Halfway between the Full and New Moon is Hecate's time to craft magic and tie up loose ends. It's also a powerful time in the lunar cycle for transitions. Balance is the key! The darkness and light dance in seamless synergy during this period.

KEYS TO THE CROSSROADS RITUAL

When you need to make an important decision, create an altar honouring Hecate. Decorate it with magical treasures and include a key or something similar as an offering to the shadow queen. When the moon appears from behind the shadows, light a candle and intuitively reflect on the best path to take. You can then step forward with poise, knowing Hecate and her hounds have your back. You've got this!

CROSSROAD SPELL CHANT

The shadowy moon above me, the mysterious Underworld below me, Hecate's torchlight before me, Hecate's hounds behind me, the wisdom and strength of the great Goddess within me. So, mote it be.

ARTIST PROSE

Raw violet stares in queendom three
Of moon and moon and moon
The mist de-veils and darkness shines
Of mysteries shed of musings mask
Truths unfurl in triple chants
Of two and yet of three
With hues of then and shades of now
Paths arcane in secrets shown
Silken threads yet hidden
Reveals, they wait for you ...

HANWI'S MOON TEMPLE: DAKOTA (OČETI ŠAKOWIŊ)

MOON GUIDE

Hanwi is the moon spirit in the culture of the Očeti Šakowiŋ people of North America. Her name means 'night sun'. She is the spirit of motherhood, kinship, natural cycles and feminine power, as well as a space holder for women during their monthly moontime and during periods of transformation. Hanwi is the wife of the sun, Wi, and together they create harmony and balance. She is the evening light, while he is the morning light.

PERSONIFICATION

Hanwi represents the rhythm of moon cycles, fertility, dreams, intuition and purification. Her energy, derived from the moon, is said to pierce like an arrow through the darkness and relieve any self-doubt or fear. The spirit of Hanwi stands for creation, freedom, willpower, bravery, authenticity and inspired action.

TOTEMS

The moon or 'night sun' is her chief symbol. White wolves, horses, feathers and phases of the moon also come into play. These signify her strong connection to the earth's elements, seasons and natural cycles.

ROOTS

The Očeti Šakowiŋ are an ancient, wise and profoundly spiritual people. There are three main groups in the upper Midwest of America today: the Dakota to the east, the Lakota to the west, and the Yankton and Yanktonai between them. The black hills of South Dakota are the spiritual heart of the Očeti Šakowiŋ. The path and cycles of the sun, stars and people are followed and celebrated here.

FOLKLORE

Hanwi's husband, the sun god Wi, is said to have dishonoured her by becoming infatuated with an earthly woman and then further rubbing salt in her wounds by inviting her to take Hanwi's seat in the sky. Hanwi often hides part of her face in disgust, resulting in the different phases of the moon. When the sun is furthest away, Hanwi bravely faces her husband, and we have a Full Moon.

MOON-HONOURING TRADITIONS

In Očeti Šakowiŋ tradition, when a woman is menstruating or on her 'moontime', it's a sacred time for rest, renewal, cleansing and going within for deep transformation. Women are believed to be at their most powerful during this time. Under Hanwi's Dark Moon, it is the perfect time to cleanse and release any unwanted energy.

17. SHELTER

*I relax in the warm comfort
of the moon mother.*

MOONLIT CODEWORDS

Hide, Conserve, Purify

MOONBEAM INSIGHT

Dear wild moon child, when unexpected challenges arise, ask Mother Hanwi to guide you home.

You are being called to return to your spiritual hiding place — an energetically powerful place where you feel safe and protected. This will often be somewhere in nature that sings to your spirit.

Amongst the beauty of the trees, flowers and birds, you are nestled in the warm bosom of Goddess Hanwi. Her reassuring hug encircles you. She encourages you to appreciate where you are in your life right now. Be grateful and trust in the universal plan for your bright future. Every step in your life prepares you for the next one. So be reassured, where you are now is preparing you for your next adventure.

It is up to you to bloom where you are planted. To truly blossom, put away your cares, rest, build up your strength and realign to your still centre and solid core. Preserve your precious energy and save it for meaningful moments that sing to your soul. Focus on the beauty all around you and witness the flowers of optimism unfurl in your flourishing garden. Bloom through the crevices and cracks to grow towards the radiant moon and sunlight.

This card may also mean a happy move is on the horizon for you. This could be a new home or workplace. Either way, an exciting venture awaits you. Step into this fresh phase with gusto. Like the perpetual cycle of the moon, change is inevitable, but growth is optional. Grow through the seasons to flourish and flow. Follow the path of least resistance to find your rhythm and dance with the moon and stars.

Go where you feel most supported and appreciated for your unique contribution and quirky personality. Your soul-aligned community will resonate with your innate essence. Love-minded souls celebrate each other's success and lift each other up in times of need. Your people are out there and waiting for you.

MOON GUIDE: HANWI

In Očeti Šakowiŋ spirituality, Hanwi is a moon goddess who protects her people at night. She can hide under her magical cloak whenever she chooses — which explains why the moon has different phases. She represents feminine cycles and the rites of passage for women.

MOON PHASE: FULL MOON

The Full Moon is the divine moontime to open and embrace the light and the insight of Spirit, to come home to your inborn wisdom. Research has shown that we actually sleep less on the night of the Full Moon, so make sure you take care and look after yourself during this lunar phase.

FULL MOON RITUAL

Light a candle to amplify the cleansing power of the Full Moon. Intention is key to purifying and activating your home or office energetically. Cleanse away negative energy and invite in positive energy. Thank Goddess Hanwi for her spiritual support.

SHELTER SPELL CHANT

Great Spirit, I call on Hanwi, the blossoming moon mother. Gossamers of silver threads, kindling of desire, weave a protection cloak made of earth's fire. I wrap this cloak good and tight to shelter and protect me each day and each night. It is done in gratitude and grace.

ARTIST PROSE

Feathered blue of magics peer enfolds in fervent light
Child of deep spring fields aglow reach keeper's ardent watch
Embracing stones of cobalt shine untainted and of Moon
Revealing secrets suckled full in loves and vivid reach
Eyes closed enchanted soul of charms in scented airs beknown
Feeding heart of richer sight be heard of Nature's soul
In harboured own and nurtured held in love
The core of you is one ...

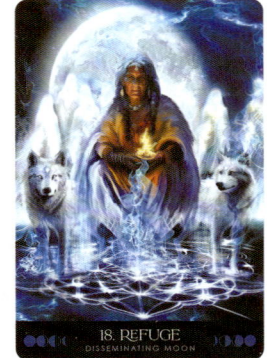

18. REFUGE

My breath is here to support me.

MOONLIT CODEWORDS

Detach, Encircle, Relinquish

MOONBEAM INSIGHT

It's time to rest and reset in the serenity of the night. Seek sanctuary with grandmother moon.

Trust in the 'night and day' of sacred balance to restore your equilibrium. Allow yourself to enjoy this downtime. You may feel some resistance to taking life at a slower pace. Give up the internal struggle and flow freely into a more harmonious state of bliss.

In the stillness of the night, a web of creative light, cleansing smoke and ancestral guides surround you in an impenetrable shield of loving protection. Along with Hanwi's two white wolves by your side, know that you are safeguarded at all times.

As a spirit animal, the wolf symbolises fierce protection, devotion and unity. In Očeti Šakowiŋ culture, the wolf is traditionally valued as a spiritual guiding force. Wolves are highly intuitive and have a mystical instinct that can detect and avert danger. You have this same inborn awareness to predict and gracefully sidestep any hazards along your life path. The wolf teaches you to feed the love, not the fear, to preserve your peace of mind. Listen to the words of wisdom that your soul whispers to you when all is quiet. Have confidence in your raw instincts to guide you onwards and upwards.

Develop a strong and harmonious relationship with yourself. Gift yourself a 'home, sweet home' to house your spirit. Remember the very best relationship you can have is the one you have with yourself. So back yourself, stop the internal self-loathing and start loving all of you. Accept and embrace your light and shadow. Strengthen your self-love to build an aura of confidence that repeatedly attracts goodness to you.

Healthy detachment brings a comforting sense of freedom. Set your soul free by releasing toxic ties that restrain and drain you, where you can.

MOON GUIDE: HANWI

Grandmother wolf offers reprieve, guidance and warm lodging from life's storms under her cloak of protection. As the wise elder she encourages you to fiercely protect your boundaries and to return home to your heartland when you are in need of loving support and wise counsel.

MOON PHASE: DISSEMINATING MOON

The disseminating phase is connected with breaking unhealthy attachments from your life. When you understand how to weave the wisdom of discernment into the fabric of your life, you fortify your boundaries, so you feel grounded and safe as houses.

DISSEMINATING MOON RITUAL

Place this oracle card on an altar dedicated to the moon. Light a candle, breathe and listen to shamanic drumming music. Drum and howl in honour of Hanwi's fierce love. Drum away what no longer serves you and call in the loving protection of the grandmother wolf.

REFUGE SPELL CHANT

Great Spirit, I call to the ancestors, hear my welcome song. Bless my heart, bless my home, bless all that seek safe refuge, and so it is.

ARTIST PROSE

Encircled love thrums the night sun's baying
Re-echoes Grand-Ancients of fierce blood and evermore spirit
Padded footfalls boundaries alight with visions and crowning fangs
Running untethered in the chambers of infinite heart
Knowing wisdoms intoned holds space
Resounding branches of inherited forests of inner vessels of life
Humming medicines of elders' past
Offering shelter of yielding and sight of Threeness
Into roots of Earth and Light
The returning of you …

19. RHYTHM

*My moon dance twirls and whirls
in divine timing.*

MOONLIT CODEWORDS

Flow, Synchronise, Pulsate

MOONBEAM INSIGHT

Presently, there is a coordinated rhythm about your life. Everything is falling into place easily for you.

Like the moon, all creation has an endless rhythm of cycles and seasons. Everything has an intelligence, energy and frequency. As you align to the elements of nature and connect with the creative vibration of the universe, a continuous stream of natural resources and riches flow effortlessly to you. Call for your spirit animals and guides to lead you. Feel the pulse of the moon and the heartbeat of the earth. The universe is conspiring to open up channels of peace and unity and bring unbounded happiness to you.

Keep it simple, do not overthink it! Gracefully soar with Spirit. Do not force the winds of change. Reflect on the ways in which you are pushing up against the inevitable. Relinquish the need to force things to happen. Allow everything to unfurl in nature's timing. Walk softly on the earth, adapt to your environment and bend like the trees in the wind to find your sweet spot.

Keep your song from Spirit alive! Sing at the top of your lungs to reawaken your primal instincts and inborn strengths. Your intuition always knows the easiest and most fruitful way forward. Dance, weave, shake, rattle and chant around your sacred fire to ignite and invigorate your wild and free spirit. Rewild in nature to sense your way with total ease and certainty. Remember your ancestral roots anchor you to the everlasting heartbeat of the earth mother. Recall your inherent knowledge and connection with universal wisdom to breathe in unison with all life, as we are all one.

MOON GUIDE: HANWI

Hanwi is the moon spirit in Očeti Šakowiŋ mythology. She represents the perpetual phases of the moon and life cycles. She personifies the rites of passage from precious child to teen-warrior to life giver to chief and lastly, to the wise elder.

MOON PHASE: ALL MOON PHASES

The perpetual rotation of the moon signifies the cycle of life — birth, death and rebirth. Metaphorically, all the moon phases embody the phases of the feminine cycle; both the lunar cycle and the feminine bleeding cycle take around twenty-nine days.

ALL MOON PHASES RITUAL

Connecting with the phases of the moon can bring awareness to your own natural rhythms. You may wish to journal your insights, feelings and reflections over a lunar month to synchronise with the powerful manifestation energy of the moon.

RHYTHM SPELL CHANT

I ebb and flow, rise and fall with the ocean tides. I wax and wane, glow and grow with the moon. I dance in a circle freely in time with the wild ones.

ARTIST PROSE

Eons vast and spinning turns for age and agelessness
Celestial earth and grounded skies the seasons everlast
Unending beat of hearts of one in moving realms become
Fluttered felt of gentlest touch on wings of patterned ways
Benighted streams of dusted lines skirt golden hues and shades
Pulses dance upon the drifts of tides
Wilderness of circling feels not once but synchronised
Suckled cores and spirit hearts, their essence they ensue
Measured beats of re and wild their cadence it relates
Empowers evolution, it sways forever you …

20. INSIGHT

My spirit glows brightly like the night sun.

MOONLIT CODEWORDS

Observe, Unearth, Ignite

MOONBEAM INSIGHT

Hanwi, the fire lighter, sparks your imagination and ignites your inner fire!

Your creativity is ablaze for you at present. Open to receive the many bright ideas and intuitive messages sparking within you. Inspiration and wisdom can be found within the seasons and lunar cycles. Open your eyes to see the synchronicities. Take note of the signs and symbols hidden in mother nature all around you. Intuitively interpret these visions to make them relevant and meaningful for you.

Harmonise your own inner rhythm with the pulse of the moon. Release control and surrender to the flow of nature's cycles. In this spiral of sweet surrender, inspiration streams in smoothly and portals of creative light and intuitive consciousness are opened to you.

Focus on your burning desires and consciously create your life. You have the power within. Your blazing inner flame grows by stoking the fire of your passions. Don't dim your dazzling moonlight for anyone or anything. Shine bright! Trust that your authentic gifts are wanted and needed in the world.

You are divinely protected. Invoke Hanwi, the Warrior of the Moon, along with your own inner rebel to shield you from all adversity. Hanwi's moonlight illuminates the darkness and radiates more power than the sun. Her moonlight and scented smoke protect you from any harm. It is safe to gleam and beam as bright as the night sun.

MOON GUIDE: HANWI

Hanwi is the soothsayer, visionary and spiritual messenger of the Očeti Šakowiŋ culture. She is all-seeing and all-knowing. Her name translates to 'night sun'. *Han* means 'darkness' and *Wi* means 'sun'. The wise Očeti Šakowiŋ are an ancient and highly spiritual people.

MOON PHASE: NEW MOON

The New Moon signifies the beginning of a new lunar cycle. It is the ideal time to get crystal clear about your 'why'. When you know your 'whys and wherefores' the universe conspires to co-create with you.

NEW MOON RITUAL

Welcome the new! Clear your space with fragrant smoke. Go to an open window or door and fan away the stagnant energy. Trust that a simple ritual of gaining clarity around your intentions, creating space to honour them and then sending them out into the cosmos is sufficient.

INSIGHT SPELL CHANT

May my being and space be infused with cleansing smoke, so I can release what is no longer serving me. May my spiritual sight be purified and activated, so I can see the signs and interpret their deeper meaning. And may the scented mist carry my wishes to Hanwi, the night sun, for inspiration.

ARTIST PROSE

Lunula peers with whispers gleam
From the shadows broad she alights
Foreshadows oath of celestial highs caressed
On butterfly wings and patterns adorned
Through flame, through sage, through yielded thrill
In unseen mysteries arise
In baying of fire and scented howls
The sacred they ascend in sight
The sooth of saying in sense of knowing
Yon blazing wise is yours ...

HINA'S MOON TEMPLE: HAWAI'I

MOON GUIDE

Graceful and beautiful Hina is the Hawaiian goddess of the moon. Her themes are lunar, natural and feminine cycles. She also oversees relationship resolution and cooperative mediation. She is a big supporter of the vulnerable and champions equality. As a wayshower and mother spirit, she inspires creative pursuits and soulful adventures, and grants flourishing new growth, intuition and creativity.

PERSONIFICATION

Hina is the embodiment of the moon and ocean, which have a co-creative relationship. She is a powerful feminine force, goddess and queen. Her name means 'grey like the moon', and 'silver like moonbeams'. Hina can refer to multiple different feminine aspects and is closely linked with female fertility and good causes.

TOTEMS

Hina's rainbow signifies the spiritual connection between the moon and the earth's oceans. Her symbols are silver and white lunar-coloured items including plants, stones and coconuts. Coral and ocean treasures are also her sacred ritual objects.

ROOTS

Traditional Hawaiian beliefs encompass the presence of ancestral spirits, deities and vitalities in natural elements, like the waves, moon, sky and ocean. Many of these spiritual values and ideologies continue today. *Mahina*, the Hawaiian word for the moon, originates from Goddess Hina. She marks a long tradition of the Hawaiian people across numerous islands. Near the mountains of Hilo, close to the ocean, hollow hills covered in lush greenery are Hina's natural sanctuary and sacred site.

FOLKLORE

One day, Hina decided to leave the ocean depths and trek up a rainbow into the sky. She went to the sun but found it so hot and uncomfortable that she could not live there. The next night, she climbed the rainbow to the moon and was so happy with what she found that she made it her forever home.

MOON-HONOURING TRADITIONS

The sacred drumming of the traditional *ipu* gourd beats across the Hawaiian islands, sea and sky as Hina and her people chant to the akuas (spirits) of the moon, "*Mahina o hoku, Ho'ike a'e 'oe, A I kou nani*," meaning, "Full Moon of the night, reveal your beauty."

21. CULMINATION

I grow and thrive in times of change.

MOONLIT CODEWORDS

End, Reawaken, Renew

MOONBEAM INSIGHT

Breathe deeply, stay calm and grounded to the earth as events reach a climax. In this card, the mounting of the Balsamic Moon has reached its summit in the shadowy night sky. You are nearing the culmination point or completion of a cycle. Surrender to the moon mother during this end phase as you complete the final stage.

It may be that you are about to reach an exciting pinnacle in your life. This highpoint could be an academic achievement, graduation or a breathlessly anticipated outcome. You've come a long way, now it's time to rejoice and rest as all your grit and determination has paid off. Prepare for a fresh cycle with new dreams woven in.

In the reverse sentiment, it may be a sad loss, death or ending. Relinquish any deeply rooted grief to the moon mother for healing. Set your soul free! Forgiveness removes the shackles of bitterness to transform any blackness into the light of love.

Irrespective of the meaning, this is a time to honour a long-awaited completion. It is a time to tie up loose ends, make peace with all the things you have experienced and celebrate the cycle of the new.

Endings are a chance to release obsolete patterns and attachments that no longer serve you. Letting go makes room for the next best thing. Endings are really veiled beginnings. Completion and the subsequent new chapter are simply bookmarks in your never-ending life story.

Everything is interconnected and one thing flows into another. Know that beginnings and endings all meld into the One.

MOON GUIDE: HINA

Like dewdrops caressing the ocean, the Hawaiian goddess Hina weeps tears of sweet surrender. She is the bringer of life and guardian of death. She weaves the fabric of creation and shows the way to undying love. She nurtures and holds you through the continuous sequence of death and rebirth.

MOON PHASE: BALSAMIC MOON

As the final stage in the lunation cycle, the Balsamic Moon is the monthly 'dream weaving' time. Also known as a Waning Crescent, it is the final thread of moonlight before the birth of the New Moon. This lunar sequence embodies the completion and culmination of all that has come before.

BALSAMIC MOON RITUAL

Write a list of everything that you want to release. Prepare a bowl of water and infuse with crystals, shells, petals and salt or go to the ocean if nearby. Rip up your list and place it in the water. Swirl around, wash away and with focused intention, simply let go! Repeat the chant below.

CULMINATION SPELL CHANT

Aloha! The creative insight I conceived, the dream I imagined, the higher path I shadowed, it's here within reach. I birthed life, I cultivated love, I believed. Under the mysterious shadow of the Balsamic Moon, I end this round with heartfelt thanks, I make space for renewal, and I welcome the new. Aloha!

ARTIST PROSE

Briny grief of sorrows
Spilled diamond tears of ache
Shadows wintered reach of barren fingers worn
By cradled moon she smiles with care
Echoed lives on rippled waves
Love's eternal gift brought fore
Light of cosmic realms adrift
Dwellings heart and never lost in swells of deepened sees
Transformation salted feels conserved
With the ocean swells endless and forever yours …

22. TRANSITION

I navigate change with grace.

MOONLIT CODEWORDS

Change, Adapt, Personify

MOONBEAM INSIGHT

An uprising and spiritual revolution are on the cards for you. Whether it's imposed or conscious change, this upheaval will turn your life around.

Grief disrupts your life, breaks you open and invites you to heal your heart with compassion and serenity. Take as much time as you need to fully transform the pain into peace. Cry a river, wash away the tears, breathe and go within to find your island home of healing. Slowly let the light in and begin with baby steps until you are ready to rise and blossom once more.

The ocean and the moon work in unison to create the tides of change. You are being called to follow the path of least resistance. Be flexible and flow with all the phases of the moon. Forcing things only disrupts the natural progression. Instead get lost in the ecstatic dance of creation to fly freely into the endless blue sky. Follow your heart and listen to your inner-guidance system. Sense your way and breathe a sigh of relief, knowing you are free to glide across the sea of love to new horizons.

Goddess Hina's blue hibiscus is magnificent, but its beauty isn't just skin deep. The sapphire bloom symbolises wisdom, peace and grace. It teaches you to listen to your inner voice and see with your heart to find a flicker of light in the darkness. As you embrace this transition, you will find your authentic expression unfurls intuitively. It is your time to bloom like the blue hibiscus!

As a mother goddess, Hina nurtures you through the spiral of life — through evolutionary shifts, endings and beginnings, death and rebirth. She guides you to embrace transformation, knowing that everything is cyclic, and this too will pass. Change is inevitable whereas growth is purely optional. It is your choice to evolve.

MOON GUIDE: HINA

Born on a stormy night full of mystery and intrigue, Goddess Hina prevails through tough times of transition and spiritual growth. She captures windstorms and moon rays to restore peace on earth. She declares that you have these same compelling skills and qualities. Harness your sacred power!

MOON PHASE: ALL MOON PHASES

All of Hina's moon phases are connected to the powerful force of creation. Because the moon repeatedly passes through cycles of growth and reinvention, the lunar phases are seen as cosmic codes to guide your own cycles, personal progress and evolution.

ALL MOON PHASES RITUAL

Follow and chart the moon cycles to plan and forecast your optimum times to rest, work and play. Check in with the moon each night and connect with the lunar mother to amplify your wishes and put your fears to bed.

TRANSITION SPELL CHANT

With each step, I kiss the earth, embrace the magic of the moon, harness the power of the winds and dance in time with the heartbeat of the moon mother. Blessed be the moon. Aloha, Hina.

ARTIST PROSE

Oceans blue resounding folds the rolls of ebb and flow
Caerulean waves of glittering stars in galaxies grieved and born
Grace of cherished passages, awake, awash, aware
Conscious flood in salt and briny swirls of yielded change
Under tides in cycles spun in boundless depths of dark
Illumination companions light in shifting space of tears
Knowns transformed in ways be shown treasured in open blooms
Beauty's surge is now you ...

23. DESIGN

I am a creative force of nature.

MOONLIT CODEWORDS

IMAGINE, SHAPE, FABRICATE

MOONBEAM INSIGHT

The sky's the limit! Don't put a glass ceiling on your goals. The whole shebang is possible for you. You can achieve anything if you decide to. It's up to you to dream extravagantly!

Everything you need is within reach. Just like Goddess Hina scatters her seeds on the wind like enchanted moondust, you have the essential elements to cast your gleaming vision.

Follow the goddess spiral inward and upward to realise your immeasurable capacity. It is time to harness your creative power and gather your courage to birth blossoming new beginnings. From the seeds of faith, bright blooms unfurl and dance in the radiant light.

Mould your life consciously from the sacred earth of the goddess. Hold your vision high and stay focused on your long-term vision to refill and sustain your motivation. Plant the seeds of hope and then bring your soulful offerings to life through faith in action. Surrender and synchronise with the natural phases of the moon. Time flies when you flow freely and enjoy the process of your creations.

Bring your playful inner child out to play, draw, paint and daydream. Spirited fun opens gateways of abundance and scatters your path with golden gems of effervescent joy. Delight in the riches that are revealed to you along the way.

MOON GUIDE: HINA

Celebrated as the queen of creation, Goddess Hina brings inspiration. She is the messenger of divine intervention and the vital breath of the cosmos. Dreams are conveyed on Hina's winds of change.

MOON PHASE: NEW MOON

The veil of the New Moon is a time for retrospection and discovering the unseen. It calls for stillness and mindfulness. In being fully present you can reflect on your heartfelt wishes that sometimes get lost in the flood of so much doing.

NEW MOON RITUAL

Bring a sense of intention and presence, as you surrender to the serenity of the New Moon. Spend some quality time journalling and exploring what is in your heart of hearts. Ask yourself the question, "What do I most want to summon into my life right now?"

DESIGN SPELL CHANT

I bow to the queen of creation. With her guidance I seed my intentions. I welcome tingles of delicious delight and an endless spiral of creative light. I unfurl my beautiful blossoms of love. I see my visions come alive! In flower now, I bloom and give deep thanks to glorious Hina. Aloha.

ARTIST PROSE

Invoked, the flurry of living gold bequests
Through gentle lush of seedings fall
Where skyward planes of earthen tides
Kindled growth of worships song
Dazzling hearts sung intended bloom
The regal fuelled through ancient's crown
Unbroken sparked in flourished gleam
Enthralled the heralds unfurled they ride
To tease forth coming of creations want
You are the creatrix of powers shown ...

24. JOURNEY

I am a light warrior of love.

MOONLIT CODEWORDS

Break out, Explore, Arise

MOONBEAM INSIGHT

Ride the wave of victory! An upsurge of good fortune is streaming in for you.

Bring forth your inner warrior of courage and self-belief. Be a little daring. Unleash your free-spirited rebel to lunge forward fearlessly and dive headfirst into the unknown. The moon will light your way to great heights.

One of life's greatest discoveries is that the hunt, not the prize, is the most rewarding part. Life is a sacred quest. Overcoming challenges builds your confidence, abilities and ingenuity. So, stick it out! Take a break if you need to, but never give up. The highs and lows provide contrast and balance. It keeps things interesting and gives you endless opportunities to learn and grow.

Overflowing waterfalls mean intuitive messages are flowing freely for you. Spending time in nature fortifies your intuition. Listen to your inner voice and leap with faith. Reawaken your raw instincts to revive hidden passions. Tap into all your senses to strengthen your psychic clarity and open to portals of pleasure. Don't forget to enjoy the sensations of living consciously!

This oracle message also indicates that you are a wayshower and lightworker. You walk your talk! By embodying and living your truth, you naturally inspire others. You are the awakened warrior who links the sacred waterways between the earth and moon. These canals of wisdom and knowledge inspire your higher purpose and spiritual mission.

As an eco-friendly rebel of the planet, environmental causes may come naturally to you.

MOON GUIDE: HINA

Moon Goddess Hina is the death mother, giver of life, rainbow warrior and wayshower. In her Dark Moon aspect, she presides over death. As the Waxing Moon, she is the giver of life. The name Hina means 'giving light'.

MOON PHASE: WAXING CRESCENT MOON

When the moon begins its expansion phase, it is time to commence a new pursuit. The first step towards the Full Moon inspires optimism and progression. At this time, even the most cautious people may be more likely to leap without a second thought.

WAXING CRESCENT MOON RITUAL

The focus of this ritual is to connect with whatever it is that lights you up. As you breathe in and out, sense your light body expand and merge with the sacred pulse of the growing moon. Allow your inner vision to manifest your luminous dreams in full colour.

JOURNEY SPELL CHANT

Aloha. In the heartbeat of Hina, we are all lovers. In the heartbeat of Hina, we are all One Love. I ride Hina's wave of love with immense gratitude in my heart. Aloha.

ARTIST PROSE

Expanding light of crescents swell
Heaven and earth through courage might
Time is bridged, of life, of streams, of falls
Steadfast held of quested twisting paths
Rippled valour of salted rivers and change
Through cycles of paths, of spirited ways
Nature's force and blazer's trails
Succulent life quenched creative thirst
Bearing the torch of heart explored
Into the mysteries of you ...

INANNA'S MOON TEMPLE: SUMER

MOON GUIDE

Also known as 'Lady of the Heavens', Inanna is the ancient Sumerian goddess of fertility, reproduction and sacred leadership. She is multifaceted and known as a conqueror and helper of humankind, a passionate lover and powerful creatrix.

PERSONIFICATION

Inanna embodies love, authentic sensuality, beauty, strength, divine law and sovereign power. As a shadow goddess with queenly status, her strong self-belief leads her bravely into the Underworld to return unscathed. She can invoke intense emotions in others for spiritual growth. Her goddess gift can mystically bestow good luck and longevity.

TOTEMS

As a multidimensional goddess, Inanna has many encryptions, symbols and signs, including her lapis lazuli amulet and staff, owls, lions, dogs, evening and morning stars, planet Venus, an embellished throne, wings, the Tree of Life, the *Ankh* or 'key of life', and many more.

ROOTS

Inanna's ancient temple is located at Uruk, modern-day Warka, in southern Iraq. With the rise of the Akkadians and Assyrians, she later merged into the goddess Ishtar, and subsequently the Hittite Šauška (Shaushka), Phoenician Astarte, Greek Aphrodite, Roman Venus, Egyptian Isis, Christian Mary Magdalene, among many more.

FOLKLORE

In her challenging journey into the Underworld, Inanna rouses the anger of the Anunnaki (the deities that serve as judges in the Underworld) when she boldly sits on her sister's throne, who is queen of the dead. Inanna is slain, and only with the assistance of her devoted priest is she able to come alive again and return to the world above.

MOON-HONOURING TRADITIONS

Inanna's feasts and festivals were aligned to the moon phases, stars and planet Venus. She was believed to love her food and have a sweet tooth, so offerings often included honey cakes, fruit and nuts, sweet buns and wine. When she was pleased, she would reward all with a cornucopia of abundance.

25. SENSUALITY

I open all my senses to fully experience sacredness in the flesh.

MOONLIT CODEWORDS

Soften, Open, Enjoy

MOONBEAM INSIGHT

Magical portals of desire are opening up for you!

Relax, receive and relish in the lusciousness of love — the source of your vital creativity.

Goddess Inanna inspires you to be unapologetically you! Fully embrace your exceptional beauty and unashamedly immerse yourself in your raw, primal essence. When you believe in your own worth, it casts an alluring aura all around you!

The sacred is not outside of you but found within you. It is through your precious body temple that you commune with the Divine. When you deliberately open your physical senses, your psychic abilities are heightened. Your body is a conduit for Spirit. Your sensuality is the heartbeat of the Divine pulsating within you, all around you and radiating from you.

Throughout the ages, spiritual doctrines have hinted towards the sacredness of sex. Sexual synergy has the divine power to transform and heal. Sacred sexuality may help release blocks around physical intimacy, body image and guilt-free pleasure.

It is about aligning the fire of your sexual energy, passion and desires with your heart and spirit. When these divine forces come into balance and harmony, sex becomes an alchemical process — empowering and transcendent. This cosmic dance ignites an ecstatic union and unrestrained euphoria.

By merging conscious connection with physical intimacy,

sex can also be a portal to trans-dimensional experiences and altered states of Oneness consciousness. Through sex and sensuality, you can experience ecstatic states of bliss, unity and enjoyment. Sacred sensuality is an invitation to divine love that unlocks spiritual doorways to the realm of infinite possibilities, limitless potential and miracles.

MOON GUIDE: INANNA

Inanna, the Sumerian goddess of love and passion, is strongly connected to the loved-up planet of Venus. The creative magic of her womb and primal sensual essence holds the cosmic power of the universe.

MOON PHASE: DISSEMINATING MOON

Sometimes referred to as the 'Waning Gibbous Moon', the Disseminating Moon is the time to open your senses to receive unrestrained pleasure, intuitive wisdom and intimacy on all levels.

DISSEMINATING MOON RITUAL

Journalling is a ritual for soul reflection. To get the insights flowing, start with journal prompts. Something like, "What do I need to shift and transform to fully sense and experience pleasures in my life?" Then, intuitively write the answer without censorship.

SENSUALITY SPELL CHANT

Dear Inanna, goddess of passion, I come to you pure of heart, mind and spirit. Please fill my body temple with your divine presence. Help me reawaken the sensual divinity that dwells within. I embody unrestrained sensual freedom.

ARTIST PROSE

Arousal drapes bejewelled to touch, they curl and writhe and stretch
Flourished heat unfurled and bloomed razes to the now
Trickles gold drops flowing swells aflame
Sacred raw and roar they pulse
As one and all in gilded bliss of breath and life undone
With dreams embraced and honour known
High spirit thrives in fullness leaves
Entwined in regal floods a-bud
Emboldened bare in temples ease alight in endless you ...

26. SHADOW

I love my light and darkness.

MOONLIT CODEWORDS

Embrace, Reframe, Accept

MOONBEAM INSIGHT

This is a time of deep healing for you. You are being called to descend into your unconscious, recover what you have denied about yourself and learn to love your shadow. Goddess Inanna is here to reassure you that this quest to the Underworld is a pathway to wholeness.

Your shadow self is made up of those facets that your social programming has told you are undesirable. Although it's not an easy process, shadow work has the capacity to transform embedded pain into peace and help you reach a sovereign sense of wholeness in your life. Whether it's your hidden desires, grief or even your rage, you are being called to fully accept your dark side.

Deep self-honouring is having compassion for whatever you perceive within yourself as both light and dark, right and wrong, good and bad. Free yourself by stripping away any self-imposed restraints to reveal your naked truth and raw vulnerability. Reawaken the dormant parts of yourself and the pieces hidden away to restore your equilibrium. Remembering the parts that make the whole brings everything back into harmonious balance.

Take your time! The spiral into the darkness to integrate your shadow can take on a life of its own. You can't rush the process. When you bypass the steps, you only delay the healing.

It's not easy, but it's worth it. Like the phases of the moon, draw comfort knowing that all cycles come to an end including the challenging ones. You will ascend out of the darkness and into the light and emerge much different to who you thought you were when you left. Stronger, wiser and feeling far more like the real you.

You may have already been in the Underworld for a while doing the deep inner healing work. In this case, the presence of Inanna is a sign that it's time to rise into the light of a new day.

MOON GUIDE: INANNA

Inanna, Sumerian Queen of Heaven, journeyed to the Underworld where she was stripped bare and left for three nights. Inanna was only allowed to leave if she found a replacement. She chose her deceitful sun-lover, Dumuzi, who, in her absence, had seized her throne of Heaven.

MOON PHASE: DARK MOON

The Dark Moon is like a cosmic sigh. A time to integrate everything you learnt in the closing moon cycle. It is where the real growth transpires. This is where the wisdom of the last moon cycle assimilates into your soul.

DARK MOON RITUAL

Shadow work for the Dark Moon journal prompts:
- What insights did you receive in this closing moon cycle?
- What are you celebrating this lunar month?
- What life lessons and wisdom are you taking forward into the next moon cycle?

SHADOW SPELL CHANT

I am now free to come out from behind my shadow to shine like the sun, glow like the moon, flow like water and grow like the earth!

ARTIST PROSE

Shadow calls through winter's wise of darkest moon
Inanna cloaked in sovereign self of truth she unbinds
Her caress, the depths of conscious revolution
Piercing sight of clarity borne through inspired streams
Her liquid-gold rivers quickening velvet blues of under-earth
Enfolded swathes of clandestine cloaks
Brave of sight, of accordant splendours
Moon goddess of shadowed depths unplumbed
And through her reframed mists of change
You are your awakening.

27. TEMPLE

My soul is ready to live the life of my dreams.

MOONLIT CODEWORDS

Open, Ask, Listen

MOONBEAM INSIGHT

The Temple of Inanna holds the divine plan that guides the creation of all life. Inside, her devotees hold and pour vessels of life-giving water continuously onto the earth. You have the power to harness this same lifeforce energy with intentional focus and foresight.

It is time to dedicate yourself to spiritual growth, purification and transformation. Walk the walk and talk the talk! Align your intentions, decisions and actions to your core values and highest vision for your life. Your top priorities need to be in alignment with your desired outcome. Consciously harmonise your sphere and overcome any obstacles by removing the things that stand in your way.

The sacred purpose of life is to be a channel for divinity on earth, a temple of wisdom. As a living temple and heavenly channel, your body serves as a bridge between worlds, a place where sacredness dwells. You are able to draw down sacred energy from the heavens above and access the powers of creation and manifestation that flow through you.

Get into your body and awaken your intuitive senses to communicate with your inner wisdom. Your crown chakra, at the softest part of your skull, is actually a portal where your 'wings of light' unfurl, enabling you to access higher streams of wisdom and your inborn gifts. Your heart is the vessel of your soul — accessing your heart wisdom illuminates your intuitive-feeling sense. Seeing is believing! Activating your third eye, clarifies your inner vision and brings your dreams to life.

When you sharpen your intuitive senses, your manifestation power surges. If you can see, feel and know your dreams are coming true, it is already done. Upgrade your beliefs, trust the process, focus on the present and remain unwavering in your belief. See it, feel it, know it and it will come your way.

MOON GUIDE: INANNA

Goddess Ishtar, alongside Venus and Aphrodite, emerged from Inanna's ancient lineage. Ishtar was also known as the Queen of Heaven and became one of the most celebrated divinities in the Sumerian pantheon, with flourishing temples across Mesopotamia.

MOON PHASE: FULL MOON

The Full Moon illuminates the shadow consciousness within. Like Inanna's starlight, the radiant moon shines light onto the darkness. It is the divine time to receive healing, manifest magic and look at what is being reflected back to you.

FULL MOON RITUAL

Make yourself an Inanna wand for lunar magic. Find a rose branch or a fallen tree twig and let it dry. Embellish it with crystals or anything that feels meaningful to you. During your Full Moon rituals, point your wand towards the heavens to invoke Inanna's star power.

TEMPLE SPELL CHANT

I pray that I may serve this divine life that sustains and preserves me. I affirm my highest desires with all my body, mind and heart.

ARTIST PROSE

Sacred star and lover's line through ancient realms commands
Ignites in arcs of graceful flush of temples mysteries grown
Beatific wings of diamonds earth inground with bless-ed step
Lunula filled with magics crowned in sweeping starlight dust
Cascades of molten radiance in justness heralded boom
On bellows roared the asking heard and listened deeply seen
Unfurling blue in spans of endless life
Immortal mystics kindled whole of rites and hallowed prayers
On priestess high you shall transcend on nigh ...

28. VISION

I see the highest vision of unity for the planet.

MOONLIT CODEWORDS

Unify, Inspire, Guide

MOONBEAM INSIGHT

Opportunities to unite and encourage a global community are opening up for you.

Trust in yourself! You've got what it takes to lead from the heart and create an inclusive environment for everyone to flourish and thrive. Your higher purpose and calling to be of service drives you. This is your sacred mission. Remember that making a positive difference in the world happens in both little and big ways. Don't dismiss your small acts of kindness and remember every loving ripple creates a tidal wave of love.

Sacred leadership starts with a great vision. This can be both your personal 'why' and higher purpose for the collective that brings universal hope. Your collaborative and compassionate style makes you a natural at guiding others. Instead of an ego-centric 'me' attitude, a conscious leader embodies all aspects of an inclusive 'we' approach. This approach to leadership encompasses knowing yourself, your own backyard and the planet.

Envision what you want your life to look like without any limitation. You have the gift of intuitive sight. Seeing the invisible is a psychic superpower that opens portals of universal wisdom and aligns you directly to the Divine. Your connection to higher streams of consciousness is expanding for you. Your spiritual growth is awakening your extra-sensory gifts. Cultivate these gifts by opening your mind's eye to foresee the lessons, blessings and consequences in pathways moving forward.

Revelations roll in when you consciously seek the deeper meaning and higher learning in life's experiences.

MOON GUIDE: INANNA

Inanna is the ancient Mesopotamian goddess of divine vision, law and justice. She guides you to see the bigger picture and seek more meaningful connections. She has big plans for you and the planet. Soul-unity, equality and equity are her higher purpose.

MOON PHASE: NEW MOON

The New Moon activates a fresh perspective, a new way of doing things and a clean slate. This phase is the perfect time to sweep away the cobwebs of the mind to start anew. A lighter, more optimistic energy lifts you up to actualise your extravagant dreams.

NEW MOON RITUAL

Allow the goddess to give you guidance through the intuition of your higher self. This practice is called 'spiritual visioning'. Relax into a light meditative state and ask your question of the goddess. Open your mind and hear the voice of Inanna as she answers you.

VISION SPELL CHANT

Powers of the night and goddess bright, I summon thee. By the New Moon light, my intuitive sight is open, as this charm is now spoken.

ARTIST PROSE

She hears in night and feels through new
The moon with darkness danced
Of grace be guide to the He and his, the wings of visions throne
Through lapis lazuli the thundered skies and sounding hooves reach
Dragon sworn and horned bull empowered temple quakes
Flash of sword, light of dreams be guards of force in form
Peace intent of lion's heart of beam and ray of light
Consciousness and wings as one
Desires of truth and yours
Flown by night in dreaming's realm the insight it is you …

JACIRA'S MOON TEMPLE: BRAZIL

MOON GUIDE
Jacira, or Jaci, is the 'Mother of All' in Tupi-Guarani culture. She is an ancient deity from the maternal Tupi ancestry. Her name literally means 'honey and moon'. As the sweet and kind-hearted moon mother, she is believed to have given birth to the River Amazon and to all life forms. She is often depicted as a beautiful mermaid and river goddess.

PERSONIFICATION
Jacira is the embodiment of the luminous moon, illuminating the night, igniting the light within and bringing gentleness and tranquillity to the world. She is the mother of fruitfulness, a bright luminary of the night and a protectress of animals, plants, lovers and the Amazon. She is a peaceful activist and harmoniser who observes situations before jumping in.

TOTEMS
In unison with the sun god Guaraci, Jacira represents sacred union. Her flourishing river symbolises fertility, her blue veil implies a state of grace, and her silver moonbeams awaken the darkness.

ROOTS
Three cultures are deeply ingrained in modern-day Brazilian spirituality — Tupi-Guarani (Brazilian), Yorùbá (African) and Catholic (Portuguese). These different cultures have shaped Brazil's modern customs and beliefs. Although Jacira is a mother goddess from the traditional Tupi-Guarani language tribes, she has integrated African and Portuguese influences over time. Jacira's natural sacred site is the River Amazon.

FOLKLORE
There are a few different versions of the sun and moon in Tupi-Guarani legend. In one of the stories, it is said that Jacira is a goddess so gorgeous that when the sun god, Guaraci, was awakened by her dazzling moonlight, he fell instantly in love with her. Their story is one of unrequited love because they cannot be together very often. Due to their 'night and day' time zones, they can only reunite briefly at sunrise, sunset or during a solar eclipse.

MOON-HONOURING TRADITIONS
The Tupi-Guarani have a sophisticated system of beliefs about the cosmos. Their shamanic rituals are influenced by the sun, moon and earth interconnection. Their music, dance and dynamic festivals rotate around natural cycles and seasons, including the moon.

29. CREATION

I am a powerful creator.

MOONLIT CODEWORDS

Build, Refine, Grow

MOONBEAM INSIGHT

Divine love is in the air! Creative dreams are wafting in for you. Breathe life into your soulful creations with magical intention.

This card signifies the start of something wonderful. Momentum is building and inspired action is generating a rainbow spiral of miraculous light. Your contagious enthusiasm and joy for the creative process propels you upward and onward.

The sacred breath of Goddess Jacira infuses your imaginings with her creative essence. Her totem, the hummingbird, may be tiny but powerful and reminds you not to underestimate something because of its size. Even the smallest idea carries immense creative power!

Blow away the cobwebs from your mind and heart that hold you back from your magnificence. Release negative self-talk and reframe with positive thoughts and feelings. It's time to surrender any perceived blocks to the creative force of the moon for transmutation.

Ask yourself, "What might I have overlooked?" Listen, observe and become fully aware of intuitive messages guiding you towards your creative vision. Hone your skills and tweak your systems and methods along the way to support your success and inspired flow.

Jacira's rainbow is also a sign of hope — the calm after the storm, the pot of gold at the arch's end. Her rainbow transmits inclusivity and diversity, an all-embracing image of love and friendship. Count your blessings! Appreciation is the goddess' way of imbuing your sacred quest with love, grace and gratitude.

MOON GUIDE: JACIRA

Brazilian goddess Jacira is known as the 'Mother of All'. One of her archetypes is the creatrix. Her name, originating with the indigenous Tupi people of Brazil, is made up of two Tupi words: *ïasy*, meaning 'moon', and *ira*, meaning 'honey'. Honey is the sweet nectar of the goddess.

MOON PHASE: FULL MOON

Brimming over with sweet promise, Jacira's Full Honey Moon accelerates your soulful offerings. It's time to inhale life's infinite potential. This phase refers to the early stage of any new relationship or fresh enterprise where everything is exhilarating and captivating.

FULL MOON RITUAL

Water is the life force that quenches your spirit, symbolising wisdom and awareness. Take the time to give thanks for this precious element. In small sips, drink in the spiritual essence of water with the intention of healing, purification, wellness and peace.

CREATION SPELL CHANT

The sacred breath of inspiration fills up my cup and water streams freely with transformative rainbow light. I drink Jacira's sweet lunar honey of love. I trust in my creations.

ARTIST PROSE

Sacred breath through drifted blush
Expressions moved in motions shift
Alchemy born creations pulse
Of fluttering time and saline jewels
Fractal light of crystals song
Deep above and light below is wept
Moon consciousness meld in natures cause
Vibrated wings of infinitude
Seeds stars awash with you …

30. BIRTH

I surrender to my infinite creative flow.

MOONLIT CODEWORDS

Begin, Preserve, Deliver

MOONBEAM INSIGHT

Feel it in your waters. The miracle of life is growing inside of you. This may be the birth of a child, sacred assignment or fertile beginning. Hold your precious babies tight! Cherish your unborn baby, soulful offerings or precious inner child. Cultivate seeds of new life with tender loving care all the way through to fruition.

Into the wild you go! In the wilderness your fierce instincts take over. Rewild to remember! Sometimes you have to forget what you think you know to remember who you really are.

You are being called to come home to your true nature — to stay true to your roots, origin and heritage. Your soul memory is reawakening to reveal your naked truth. Bare and vulnerable, and stripped of all falsehoods, your authentic self shines bright like the luminous moon. Wear your warrior scars with pride as these are the markings of the life battles that you have won. These valuable life lessons support your new beginnings from conception to birth.

You carry the magic of the moon and stars within you. Everything you need to know is already inside of you. Surrender to your wild and raw intuition and allow your natural rhythm to flow like the bountiful Amazon River.

The womb of the universal mother is the gateway to all creation. The womb is where the sacral chakra is located, the energy centre of creativity as well as wisdom and desire. This is the home of one's sweetness! You can heal the womb by sweetening your life. Learn to flow with life, honour your emotions and open up to pleasure and creativity to restore your sense of ecstatic bliss.

MOON GUIDE: JACIRA

Tupi wisdom speaks of Jacira giving birth to the Amazon River and all creation. Let's acknowledge the Tupi-Guarani language groups as the traditional custodians of central Brazil, Paraguay and surrounding areas. Their deeply rooted culture is still flourishing today.

MOON PHASE: NEW MOON

Being born on a New Moon means your life is going to be sweet like honey. It means you are adventurous, passionate and creative. During this phase, the night sky shadows the moon, even so its potential is infinite.

NEW MOON RITUAL

Listen to the wisdom of your body to create higher awareness. With eyes closed, focus just below your navel. Place your palms here and breathe. Ask, "What do you want me to know?" Reflect on the answers without judgement.

BIRTH SPELL CHANT

Moon Woman, hold me in your loving embrace. Wave after wave, the rhythm of creation births new life. I am open to receiving the mystery, magic and miracle of creation. I drink the sweet honey of love. I don't overshadow my light. I give thanks for life.

ARTIST PROSE

Advent rise returns in fertile moon she swells
Sparkling currents of painted paths expand in showing love
Deeper life of fullness knows
The seed the egg the quickening
Resounding waves vibrance lives open graceful vows
Light teased in sensual now and knowing
Cosmic winds of luscious ways
Uplift in grounded waters felt
The nurturing rings through instinct and bone
Wilds they call sacred-nest for you ...

31. GRACE

I cultivate beauty in my life.

MOONLIT CODEWORDS

Brighten, Unmask, Seek

MOONBEAM INSIGHT

You are building a better and more beautiful future for yourself.

It is by divine grace that you are able to see the opportunities and breaks available to you. Love, beauty and joy is increasing in your life. By focusing on the good in the world, you entice more positivity to you.

You carry yourself with a calm and graceful elegance. Your soul light radiates from the inside out, lighting the way for others to emulate. Your natural disposition to show kindness is your goddess-given grace. It doesn't mean you're perfect all the time, it means you choose to be compassionate and considerate even in challenging interactions and situations.

Flying off the handle, judging everything and focusing only on the 'doom and gloom' is not the way of beauty and grace. Honour your ethics. Don't get dragged into conversations that judge or shame others because it will only drain your light-force energy. In a world where you can choose to be whatever you want, choose to be kind. This naturally draws like-hearted souls and ascension pathways to you. Love breeds love.

This card may also indicate that a reunion or a twin flame reignition is on the cards for you. Physical attractions are common, but multidimensional connections are rare. A sacred union is the coming together of the physical, emotional, cognitive and spiritual facets. A divinely inspired relationship has deep intimacy on all levels.

Your capacity to love shines so bright, acting as a lighthouse for a higher love to find its way to you with ease. Know that you are whole and complete as you are, a relationship only enriches your life's journey. Each half of your twin soul is whole, but together you create miracles.

MOON GUIDE: JACIRA

The moon mother, Jacira, arises to brighten up the dark sky each night. She radiates so much beauty, dignity and love that when Guaraci, her sun god and twin flame, was awakened by her alluring moonlight and starlight, he fell instantaneously in love with her.

MOON PHASE: WAXING CRESCENT MOON

When the moon is snowballing under the Waxing Crescent, this is the divine time to increase your wealth mindset and call in more abundance. Love, beauty and joy is increasing in your life. Grow your positivity and radiate it out to attract more things to be grateful for.

WAXING CRESCENT MOON RITUAL

A daily walk in nature becomes a mindfulness practice where soul and Divine meet. Sense grace all around you. Nature has the power to heal, rejuvenate and guide you. By sending out light, love and gratitude, you feel palpably loved in return.

GRACE SPELL CHANT

Goddess of Grace, I embody your tender-hearted essence. I walk softly on the earth and dance gracefully across the skies. I scatter love, light and gentle power along the way. I give graciously and take only what I need. May I stroll through the world and see only its beauty. In grace, I thank you.

ARTIST PROSE

Through endless love of stardust moon
Rained opal's grit and heart of grace
The pearls of moon in skylit paths
Unveiled sheen in knowing's fell
Of fullness shine and lustres fire
In body's form of soul and brilliance raw
Seeking held in sovereigns' kind
Senses mettle in softness force
Thine goddess born internal waves
Thine goddess is you …

32. TEARS

I let go and let love in.

MOONLIT CODEWORDS

Grieve, Release, Surrender

MOONBEAM INSIGHT

Grief is part of the healing journey. You may be grieving the promise of a romantic relationship or the loss of a lover or an unrequited, one-sided love. Whatever the loss, the pain runs deep, and it may feel impossible to let go and make sense of it all right now. You are understandably heartbroken.

Bypassing the healing journey only delays the inevitable. You may be scared but you are exactly where you are meant to be. You can't run from the truth, so face your fears with self-compassion. Know that in time this grief will soften. Your heart will crack open to let the light of love stream back in. Your tears clear the way for a fresh start, but for now honour your feelings, cry yourself to sleep if necessary and breathe through the heartache.

When love means letting go it will take you on an emotional roller-coaster ride and you may struggle to find answers. Separation is not a concept that our higher self understands, so it may resist. Focus on the lessons learnt, love felt and happier memories to try and make sense of it all. You may also have to accept that you may never truly understand the hidden meaning.

Perhaps you loved with everything you had, and it wasn't enough? Know that you are always enough, worthy and deserving of a higher love. There is one answer that always rings true deep in your heart and soul. You know that love starts with self first. Once you merge with a higher love, you will see yourself everywhere. Relationships are mirrors of the soul for spiritual reflection and growth — sometimes joyful and, from time to time, extremely painful. Appreciate that love has divine duality, like the sun and the moon, light and shadow, day and night, fire and ice.

MOON GUIDE: JACIRA

It is said that Goddess Jacira cried a river because she could not see or be with her lover, the sun god, Guaraci. For when they touch, they destroy the earth with fire and floods. As eco-warriors, their undying love for the earth is immeasurable so they choose to love each other from afar.

MOON PHASE: BALSAMIC MOON

The Balsamic Moon is the darkest time of the lunar month but be reassured the New Moon is approaching. This is the monthly 'sleep time', so rest up and be soft and gentle with yourself. It's the perfect time to let go of past hurts and pivot towards a new future.

BALSAMIC MOON RITUAL

The breath is an invitation to surrender. It is connected with the universal heartbeat. Like seasons of the year and phases of the moon, the conscious breath is a perpetual rotation. Hand on your heart, bow to the breath and remember happier times.

TEARS SPELL CHANT

My tears are dewdrops of love that clear the way. I release the pain to leave it all behind. I now see through to the other side. My mind is clear and my heart wide open to let love back in. I heal with love. I release with love. I am open to love. I am love.

ARTIST PROSE

The Moon, she whispers the new is nigh
Passion lights the flooded tears
Rivers born of sorrows thirst rent in twain
Rage of streams and fires twin where duality collides
Unbroken heart is keepers' oath for sake of humankind
Through tempests ruin and battles forged
Endured in weight, in surrenders song
Of choice, not either or, but endlessly besides
Yet love as strength, as eternal soothe
Brings magic both and all
On feathers winged to you …

MÁNI'S MOON TEMPLE: NORSE

MOON GUIDE
Máni in Old Norse language means 'moon'. He steers the moon on its course, shaping the lunar phases. As Máni mirrors the light of his sister Sól, the sun goddess, he inspires and supports the sacred feminine to shine brightly for all to see.

PERSONIFICATION
Máni is the actual moon personified in Norse mythology. His special gifts include restful sleep, prophetic dreams, transformation, safe travel and the protection of defenceless people.

TOTEMS
Máni's totems are any items shaped like the moon or charms with the moon embossed. The eclipse and two wolves represent teamwork, unity and sacred duality. His chariot represents action, hourglasses represent divine timing, calendars represent the divine plan, repetitive number sequences represent synchronicity, runes represent prophecy and black obsidian mirrors represent seeing into the darkness.

ROOTS
Old Norse mythology belongs to the peoples of modern-day Scandinavia, comprised of Denmark, Iceland, Norway, Sweden and the Faroe Islands. Many think that the belief in Norse deities disappeared with the introduction of Christianity, but it actually went underground and was instead practised secretly. Norse mythology speaks of Máni as the perpetual moon god.

FOLKLORE
Máni is the brother of the sun goddess, Sól. It is believed that he and his sister are destined to die in the jaws of wolves, Sköll and Hati, at the beginning of Ragnarök, the foretold battle between the forces of good and evil. The ancient Norse believed that when the two wolves caught up with the sun and moon, they would swallow them, and as a result the stars would vanish from the sky. It would be a signal that Ragnarök was afoot.

MOON-HONOURING TRADITIONS
The ancient Norse honoured the moon with gifts, donations, or acts of kindness. Offerings to Máni would include night-blooming flowers or moonstones, diffusing peppermint essential oil, drinking peppermint tea and eating mint-flavoured treats. Any volunteer work or donations that benefit the global community would be considered an act in honour of Máni.

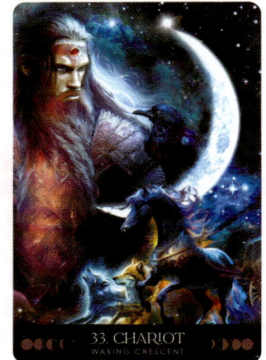

33. CHARIOT

My determination, enthusiasm and willpower pay off.

MOONLIT CODEWORDS

Act, Move, Fly

MOONBEAM INSIGHT

YES! Now is the time to go after what you really want.

The Norse god Máni inspires you to be self-disciplined and have a strong sense of direction to achieve your goals. He encourages you to plan ahead and follow through with your chosen objectives.

As the personification of the moon, Máni magnifies your determination to achieve your end target. Call on him to accelerate your get-up-and-go and propel you forward to harness your wildest dreams. Find the balance between your heart and head, to adopt a practical yet intuitive outlook to soar into the cosmos and ascend to great heights.

Your quest will not be without its challenges. There may be obstacles in your way but when you stay on track, keep your cool and are self-assured, you will continue to be highly effective. You will overcome any opposition with a problem-solving, can-do attitude. Call on Máni to approach your work and projects in a positive and deliberate way.

In love and relationships, this card heartens you to balance your emotions in order to communicate in a calm manner and reach a compromise that is a win-win for both of you. The challenges you face are easily resolved when you come together in a mutually beneficial way.

If you are healing from a broken heart, know that you can reconcile past hurts and move forward in your love life. You will rise up from this painful ending with more clarity about what you truly want in a relationship. Knowing what you do and don't want is important. This clarity will magnetise a harmonised, passionate and high-vibrational love match to you.

Another meaning indicates that travel may be on the cards for you, as the chariot is also a means of transport. Soulful escapades inspire and reawaken your sense of adventure and creativity. Don't forget to enjoy the journey!

MOON GUIDE: MÁNI

Often referred to as the 'Man in the Moon', Máni is the personification of the moon. Being the image of the moon itself, Máni is tremendously powerful. He is immortal, spirited and can wield moonbeams according to his will.

MOON PHASE: WAXING CRESCENT MOON

Máni's expanding Crescent Moon symbolises a chariot of ascension soaring through the galaxies gaining momentum as it goes. When the moon is waxing, it is a time for action and to be committed to what you are building.

WAXING CRESCENT MOON RITUAL

Create an inspirational altar. You will need a candle and a photo or keepsake that motivates you. You may choose to use this oracle card too. Find a safe space to light your candle. Place the card, picture or keepsake at the base of your candle so it is in clear line of sight to you. Recite the following spell chant with strong intention.

CHARIOT SPELL CHANT

I light this candle to bring action into my life. I consciously create my own reality without hesitation or procrastination. Máni, light the way and show me the right way even on the darkest days.

ARTIST PROSE

Sister Sun lunations cleaved alluring light of call
To reaping hook the power swells
Inspired tides forever flown
Wolves they howl on raven hues
Striking hooves, they sound
Of steeds on night and wheels they turn
Cosmic skies in motions surge across the hearted known
Enraptured sparked, enchanted flames
Through piercing gaze and clarity ways
For you they come in deeds …

34. ILLUMINATION

I am open and willing to receive clarity.

MOONLIT CODEWORDS

Shed, Extend, Radiate

MOONBEAM INSIGHT

The radiant sun goddess Sól ignites your spiritual ascent.

A lightbulb moment enlightens you to the truth! Keep your spiritual sight and heart wide open as a significant realisation is being revealed to you in a clear vision. This new understanding awakens you to the crux of the situation.

Perhaps in the past you chose not to see what was really going on because the illusion was far more appealing than the actual reality at the time. Don't beat yourself up! Instead, focus on how far you have come, appreciate the lessons and blessings, and acknowledge your awakening really will set you free. Rise from the ashes to orbit through the universe like the rising sun.

Profound spiritual awakening catapults your personal growth. Your new enlightened perspective expands your wisdom and awareness to encompass a wider, more infinite sense of reality and soul-unity. You are no longer filtering everything through your ego and just focusing on your own self-interest. Instead, you have an intuitive awareness of Oneness consciousness and the interconnection of all life.

Everyone sees life through their own lens and filter, often justifying their choices and beliefs. We each have a unique perspective of the same situation depending on our lived experience and core values. This realisation brings a more compassionate understanding and approach to others. Focus on your own learning and growth journey as you cannot influence or control anyone else's.

MOON GUIDE: SÓL

Sól is the ancient Norse goddess of the sun and sister to the moon god, Máni. She swiftly drives across the sky each day in her horse-drawn golden chariot, lighting the way for truth seekers to follow. She enlightens minds with higher wisdom and hearts with universal love.

MOON PHASE: SUN & MOON

Day and night symbolise a balanced perspective. The sun is often associated with power, positive energy and growth. While the moon is linked to intuition, mystery and transition. Together these complementary elements create symmetry.

SUN GAZING RITUAL

The sun exemplifies spiritual knowledge and a sense of oneness with the Divine. Sun gazing is a meditative practice that encompasses scrying into the rising or setting sun to help focus attention and clear the mind. Call on the sun's power to increase your connection to Source.

ILLUMINATION SPELL CHANT

In the radiance of the sunlight and shadow of the moon, Goddess Sól I call on you. Clarify my insight and help me see the light and darkness of my higher truth. So may it be.

ARTIST PROSE

Ageless Shes, they forever burn
Sisters, reshaping in endless fire and ice
Striking fingers and lapping flame sear and seer
Scorching passions of furtherance flare untethered
Yet shrouded moon of night never dousing revolution's tongue
Centres vast of infernos core
Power consuming discarded airs in transformations kiss
Hearts ablaze shines eternal
Eclipse of shadowed obscured no more
Shimmering into enchanted alchemy of self

35. IMPACT

I claim my desires as my own.

MOONLIT CODEWORDS

Pursue, Strive, Intercept

MOONBEAM INSIGHT

The moon-wolf howls her wild reassurance and declares, "Now is the time to go all out!"

It is safe to go after what you want. Now is not the time to hold back. Leap forward with gusto and confidence to capture all of the lucky breaks heading your way. *Believe in your dreams, moon child!*

Make your mark! Fully participate in your life, be generous of spirit and present in all you do. Your ravenous hunger for more passion and meaning will drive you towards your purpose. Hunt down and seize your true desires.

Abandon uncertainty and the need for validation. Do not let the naysayers or your insecurities hold you back from your own brilliance. Relinquish circumstances that no longer feel supportive or ring true for you. Waiting for unrealistic perfection only delays your plans. Embrace imperfect action to support your creative endeavours.

You are being called to get crystal clear about your top priorities so you can align your choices to match your highest vision. Like attracts like. Dance in harmony with the creative flow of the universe and weave magic in time with your natural rhythm and the moon phases to design a peace-loving and purposeful life.

Find the path of least resistance by avoiding turbulent relationships and unnecessary distractions. Have confidence, knowing all obstacles are overcome with tenacity and an optimistic outlook. Thunder forward with determination as your dreams are realised. Feel the fear and do it anyway! It takes courage to create impact. You're uplevelling right now. Love and success are coming in for you. Trust your innate wisdom.

MOON GUIDE: SKÖLL

Sköll, also known as the sun-wolf, is a warrior of love and peace. She speaks of rising above duplicity. The worst betrayal is when you betray yourself. Stay the course, follow the northern lights to your true north and oversee your own destiny.

MOON PHASE: LUNAR ECLIPSE

A lunar eclipse transpires during a Full Moon when the sun, earth and moon are all aligned. The moon shadow unveils support for you to make your move. Eclipses are culminations of emotional cycles that have run their course. It's a divine time to let go with grace and grit!

LUNAR ECLIPSE RITUAL

Eclipses are powerful catalysts for change and making space for more things to grow. It's a magical time to weed your garden, declutter, tidy up and clean out cupboards. If you need to howl at the moon during this time, cry out. Recite the impact spell below with real spirit.

IMPACT SPELL CHANT

Rays of wisdom, cosmic pulse, blessed be your synergy. United as one, shadow of the moon, light of the sun, heartbeat of the earth, guide my steps and harm no one. It is done! It is done! It is done!

ARTIST PROSE

Sól and Luna, their dance is marked
The intimacy keen and one
The dark leads forth to brighten realms
Where warrioress ways illume
Fierce sight of want and desires on quest
Veiled mysteries light of spheres
Ignite internal flames of hunt
Hoof and paw enlivened spirits roused
Flurries bring forth winter's soul to bare
Sacred aim, flies fast and true and leads her way for you ...

36. HEAD-TO-HEAD

I confront my fear head on.

MOONLIT CODEWORDS

Seize, Show, Ascend

MOONBEAM INSIGHT

Fear is a natural reaction of the mind trying to keep you safe, but in reality, it often only works to dim your light. Norse god Máni encourages you to shine your torch of wisdom brightly out into the night sky.

Máni represents strength without intimidation and leadership without force. His spirit is marked by faith in action, rational thinking and integrity. He embodies taking charge and seeing things through. He calls on you to personify these divine qualities to break through your own glass ceiling.

Be brave in that one decisive moment when fear tries to rear its head. Acknowledge the thought and feeling behind it, evaluate it and then put it into perspective. Reframe the self-sabotaging thoughtforms with a more positive frame of mind. Notice how your fear softens into the light of love.

A deep, calm inner knowing leads you in the right direction, whereas incessant worry keeps you stuck. It is up to you to discern and intuit the difference. Focus on your crowning wisdom as it will always guide you on your most aligned path.

You may be avoiding a difficult conversation with someone. Trust that conflict resolution conveys a peaceful solution for all sides. Open communication and good listening ends with a win-win outcome. Compassionate understanding and straightforwardness clear up any future miscommunication and ensures your message is received and understood with clarity and purpose.

Embrace the power of presence. When you harness the day, you appreciate the exquisiteness of the present moment and have the courage to take action and leap into your future. Enjoy the here and now, stop worrying about the past or future, just live in the moment.

MOON GUIDE: MÁNI

In old Norse mythology, Máni and his sister, Goddess Sól, work in unison to pilot the sun and moon through their pathways across the skies, endlessly chased by two wolves who symbolise their fear.

MOON PHASE: FULL MOON

The Full Moon is the phase when the sun illuminates the whole moon, making it radiate with solar power. This amplified energy can bring things to a head if not dealt with swiftly and effectively. This is a time of heightened emotions, so tread carefully to resolve conflict peacefully.

FULL MOON RITUAL

Moon bathing is quiet time spent at night basking in the glowing moonbeams. Remove yourself from any artificial light.

Set your intention to harmonise your life. Imagine the golden light of Máni's moon energetically cleansing you and your space and amplifying your intention.

HEAD-TO-HEAD SPELL CHANT

Conflict, dread and tension cease. Fear softens, I call for peace. By the power of the Full Moon and the sun. As I will it, let it be done. With harm to none, so may it be. I am whole, let me be free.

ARTIST PROSE

From darkness wings and mayhem's sway
Colliding stars transform
Knighted skies of stardust reigns
Sun-filled eyes give way to blue of night
Moon of fullness draws in strength
Cloak worn of one yet
Lone of heart hears cosmic howls
Loyalty wings on ebony shine
Mirrored in strength of pack
Yet authentically always you …

MAYARI'S MOON TEMPLE: PHILIPPINES

MOON GUIDE
Mayari is the Philippine moon goddess, protectress of Earth during the night and almighty guardian over life and death. She is referred to as 'Moon Shadow' and 'Maiden of the Moon'. As a huntress, she has her eye on the prize and always hits her target. As an enchantress, she has astonishing magical abilities to manifest miracles.

PERSONIFICATION
Mayari is the symbol of strength, courage, authentic beauty, equality, balance and fair play. She embodies the mysteries of the moon, night and shadow. She is the awakened rebel, a true visionary, who fights the good fight and wins fairly with forethought and foresight.

TOTEMS
Mayari's symbols are the sword for protection, black and white snakes representing sacred balance and rebirth, the red veil for great passion, emotional power, lifeforce energy and fortification, the golden crown for sovereign rule and higher wisdom, and the blood moon representing the beginning of the end.

ROOTS

The vibrant stories of ancient Philippine mythology encompass deities, creation stories and mythical beings. Legends differ among the many Indigenous language groups of the Philippines. Some believe in a single supreme being who created the world and everything in it, while others worship a multitude of nature deities. A version of these diverse traditions still flourishes today.

FOLKLORE

Mayari became the goddess of the moon and night after her father, Bathala, the king of the gods, died without a will. Mayari and her brother, Apolaki, fought a great battle after he denied her offer to rule Earth equally. During the clash, Apolaki struck his sister with a bamboo staff which led to the loss of her eye. He apologised and accepted his sister's proposal. She is said to rule the night, while he rules the day.

MOON-HONOURING TRADITIONS

In honour of Mayari, lovers pledge their eternal love with the moon as their witness. On the night of a Full Moon, admirers gift a floral corsage to someone they have their eye on and if that special someone wears the spray of flowers, they accept them as their lover.

37. LOVE

I create a passionate life.

MOONLIT CODEWORDS

Amplify, Embody, Appreciate

MOONBEAM INSIGHT

Your sensuality is like a love magnet. Ooze it, embody it and express it freely with self-confidence. Own your unique quintessence and love yourself as if you were a red-hot Full Moon pulsating with self-assurance and authenticity. It is your time to shine like the ruby moon and stars! Dance to your own love song to entice a higher love to you.

Be prepared to come out of hibernation and step out of your comfort zone. The best way to find a like-minded lover is to go where they hang out. Decide how you want to feel and follow that feeling. Listen to your natural instincts and soul's voice to follow a higher, happier pathway to euphoric ecstasy.

Finding your passion will help you live a full and purposeful existence. Passion, like love, is a sensation worth seeking. Do not wait for your passion to find you — look for it and create opportunities that align to your heart's desires.

Desire activates your purpose. It gives you a reason to keep seeking, learning and embracing your mastery. It opens you up to soulful experiences and spirited adventures. Passionate souls, like you, make the most of every moment. You find pleasure and simple abundance in everyday living.

Intuitive clarity grows when you open your senses to feel passion and pleasure. Self-awareness expands when you are in your body experiencing the sacred pulse of Source. The physical-body temple is a conduit for love. Let love in!

Passion knows no restrictions and being enthusiastic about

something can be explosive, like the Full Moon. Be mindful that your passion doesn't become an unhealthy obsession, that's not love. As with everything, in love there has to be sacred balance.

MOON GUIDE: MAYARI

Goddess Mayari is a timeless burning expression of desire, love and intimacy on all levels — physical, emotional, cognitive and spiritual. She ignites your inner fire of desire to live a passionate reality. She will activate your inner light of self-love and open your senses to feel delicious pleasure.

MOON PHASE: BLOOD FULL MOON

The Full Moon takes on a reddish aura when fully eclipsed. This is a time of surrendering to and welcoming pleasure into your zone. Do not rush the process, savour every scrumptious moment. Align your purpose with your passions.

BLOOD FULL MOON RITUAL

Light your candle, or fire, and gaze into the flame for a moment, allowing yourself to relax into a blissful state. Now imagine the flame burning away all the things you want to let go of, like self-loathing. Continue gazing at the flames as you reflect and imagine your deepest desires and the feelings they evoke.

LOVE SPELL CHANT

The sacred flame in my heart is ready to be ignited. I am ready to fill up on unrestrained passion. I let love in and open wide to receive tantalising intimacy. I invite passion, love and spiritual ecstasy into my sacral portal. I embrace the flames of desire. I am one with divine love.

ARTIST PROSE

Blood's tender stroke veiled flowing free
With writhing vigour arched
Through swollen lips of kinship orbed
Enflamed from crimson scarlets touched
Converge rebirthed of starry locks
Swung stirred of Loves lust lifts
Swaying wants through layered tides
Wild spirits core of centres kind laughs tears
Unfastened worth of forthright held
Love right is yours to say ...

38. PROGRESS

My life evolves at the exact right time.

MOONLIT CODEWORDS

Grow, Defend, Insulate

MOONBEAM INSIGHT

You are making progress! You may feel like it is not happening quickly enough for you, but if you go back and reflect on how far you have come, you will be pleasantly surprised about the headway you have made so far. Take the time to celebrate your small wins, ongoing advancement and ever-evolving growth to date.

You may have been so focused on the end result and achieving your goals, that you've missed the actual development of your dreams. The journey is far more rewarding than the final outcome. If you were to instantly manifest your wishes, you would miss out on rejoicing the incremental improvements and milestones along the way.

Accomplishment is not about the final destination; it is about the expedition. It doesn't mean the endpoint is irrelevant, but the journey shapes your soul's evolution. It is about who you become in the process. The path you walk has a greater role in your overall fulfilment.

It is up to you to cultivate a supportive environment where you can nurture your creative offerings through to abundant completion. Surround yourself with supportive people that encourage you and help you on your quest. Delegate and ask for assistance where possible to speed up your progress. Create collaborative connections to ensure a win-win for everyone.

Healthy boundaries will keep you focused and aligned with your divine plan. Learn to say, "No thanks" to unnecessary distractions that take you off track. Detach from negative chatter, comparison and competition. A positive mindset grows a 'can-do' attitude that supports your vision. Preserve your energy levels and repair any draining leaks that hold you back from your growth. Weather the storms with a shield of optimism and maintain a solution-based outlook to arise triumphant.

MOON GUIDE: MAYARI

Mayari is the moon goddess of humanitarian and environmental rebellions. She is also the Divine Feminine archetype of balance, equality, perseverance and patience. Call on Mayari to protect your spiritual quest and preserve your energy as you embark on your glorious adventure.

MOON PHASE: FIRST QUARTER MOON

The First Quarter Moon transpires when half of the moon is illuminated. This phase represents transition, duality and patience. An uplevel is not too far away. The best way to honour this time is to be thankful for your progress so far.

FIRST QUARTER MOON RITUAL

Find a quiet space to go within for deep self-awareness and reflection. Focus on the lessons and the blessings of your pursuit so far. Celebrate the wins and wisdom gained from your soulful expedition. Seek and intuit the helpful signs, symbols and insights to guide you onwards. Express gratitude.

PROGRESS SPELL CHANT

My slow and steady growth is still growth. Every small step inches me closer to my wildest dreams. I seek and appreciate the hidden gems along the way. I balance the light and night to delight in and enjoy my ever-evolving journey.

ARTIST PROSE

Seeker's brave of shrouded truths
Of spoken veiled in the mysteries held
Flared to bright and darkness speaks
Candour stirred through shades and hues
Of fluid skins and shedding realms
Captive faith once caged to rise and soar
While heights of grace bear strikes of swift
Of liquid light and tempered dark
The quarter she fells to even
The warrior revives through straddled sight for you ...

39. CONQUEST

I rise to the challenge.

MOONLIT CODEWORDS

Assert, Evaluate, Declare

MOONBEAM INSIGHT

Light codes activate your soul's growth. An electrifying awakening is on its way. Revelations and insights trigger your higher vision and psychic inner knowing.

What feels like a downfall or disappointment is actually a blessing and massive breakthrough in disguise. Challenges teach you to re-evaluate your priorities, reactions and boundaries. Once you are clear on your fundamentals, align your decisions and actions to fortify your happier and higher pathway. Overcoming obstacles builds your problem-solving skills and strong self-assurance. Be confident knowing you are far more resourceful and resilient now; you know exactly what you need to do.

Contrast and opposition bring to light the pros and cons of your situation. Weigh up the positives and negatives to pivot towards a brighter future. Be mindful of your thoughts and aware of your feelings as these impact your ability to rise to the challenge. Assess your next step, plan your approach and seek the best route forward.

Self-mastery is the greatest conquest! Vanquish all self-doubt, knowing that you have the power within you to conquer anything that arises in the future. Trust that whatever comes, you have the strength and skills to tackle it. Decide that no matter what comes your way, no matter how difficult or unjust, you will do more than survive, you will thrive.

Go within the indigo vortex of your mind's eye to clarify

your intuitive vision. Here in the deep well of your soul are all the answers you seek to rise to the occasion. Innovative ideas and solutions spring forth when you combine psychic insights with practical strategy. A pragmatic perspective balanced with your intuitive wisdom ensures you achieve great success.

MOON GUIDE: MAYARI

Goddess Mayari is the victor, mystic and awakener. She activates your soul's light and connection to Source wisdom. Mayari is a champion of love. She vanquishes self-doubt and teaches self-mastery. She will help you determine what you truly want and go after it.

MOON PHASE: THIRD QUARTER MOON

Spiritually, the Third Quarter Moon is a time for balancing the head and the heart. Alignment is attained when your thoughts, feelings and actions are unified with your higher purpose.

THIRD QUARTER MOON RITUAL

Mayari speaks of 'lowering your mind to your heart'. A simple practice is to begin thinking from your heart and loving from your mind. Ask your heart for guidance and, when negative thoughtforms arise, shift your focus to something beautiful. Make love the basis of your thoughts and words.

CONQUEST SPELL CHANT

I have a winner's mindset and heartset. My positive frame of mind overcomes challenges and obstacles effortlessly. I open my heart with compassion and understanding to befriend my emotions. I stop overthinking and overreacting to harmonise my life.

ARTIST PROSE

Fire's white breath, the night is split
Arouse and air rents quarter and third
Skies alight and spiralled forms
Stirred tempests to sacred heart
Twisting stars of ignited touch
Streaked evenings strength of magic dwells
Times of night be empress pledged
Warrioress
Be mine of knighted awakening
For the cosmic prowess is you …

40. BEAUTY

*Ablaze with golden rays of light,
my star quality shines bright.*

MOONLIT CODEWORDS

Bewitch, Express, Shine

MOONBEAM INSIGHT

Blessed radiant star, you have created a universe filled with so much beauty. When you see a spectacular sunset, you are reminded to treasure poignant experiences. When you help someone in need, you express the beauty within you as an act of kindness.

Goddess Mayari guides you to walk in beauty to capture the essence of your divinity. Beauty is both a path you choose to take and what frames the actual pathway. In the brilliance of creation, you see its outer beauty. In integrity and compassion, you recognise its inner expressions.

Start every day with the belief that beauty is everywhere just waiting for you to notice it. Allow yourself to sense its impact upon your soul. Some visions and observations will stop you in your tracks and take your breath away. Others will be more subtle but equally sublime. Consciously make your actions a reflection of the beauty all around you. Relish every precious moment. Stop, breathe and sense the sacredness in everything. Nourish your spirit by observing beauty in nature, simple abundance and loving moments.

The beauty of your heart is reflected on your face as it beams out from within your soul. Your authentic self is who you are at your core. It is the expression of your soul through all your quirks and strengths and provides you with genuine gratification and pleasure.

Learn the art of sharing your authentic and true essence

wholeheartedly with others. Your authenticity is the embodied alignment of body, heart, mind and spirit. Do not be afraid to share your authentic self with the world as that is what makes you beautiful to the people who truly matter.

MOON GUIDE: MAYARI

Goddess Mayari exemplifies the Divine Feminine as a powerful force which guides the soul to soar. She will help you tap into your full potential, ignite your passions and bring them to light. She is the enchantress who captivates the beauty of the glistening moon and stars.

MOON PHASE: FULL MOON

The Full Moon amplifies your authentic spirit and natural beauty. It aids you to release any self-loathing patterns and beliefs and to embrace self-loving paradigms instead. Magnify your radiant light under the Full Moonlight. Get grounded and release unwanted energy.

FULL MOON RITUAL

Look deeply at yourself in the mirror and witness your inner and outer beauty. Have an intuitive conversation with your soul's voice. Focus on your natural gifts, strengths and qualities. Look into your eyes and embrace your true self. Spend some time admiring your attributes and acknowledge what it is you love about you.

BEAUTY SPELL CHANT

On this Full Moon night, I ignite my soul light. Moonshine, starlight, infuse my body temple with love. As a flower is granted beauty, let me blossom in your light — the light that brings me true beauty and grants me life.

ARTIST PROSE

Lingers graze of sensual's brush, hypnotic veils allure,
Ethereal waves tides flush and full in regal imperial grace,
Seductions weave of moon, of primal, of wild in flame,
Sheer folds they coil and wind in delicious magics wake,
Sacred fires bare and round ignite in lust and curve,
Upon thee thine freedom of taste, of thrills,
Devoted blaze of passions embrace in bask of glories song,
Sweeps the celestial keen through you and yours,
Bewitched,
'Til you are beauty reborn ...

PHOEBE'S MOON TEMPLE: GREECE

MOON GUIDE
Phoebe has many illustrious designations. She is the daughter of Heaven and Earth, lady of the sky and mysteries of the moon, titaness of intellect, and goddess or prophet of the Oracle of Delphi. Phoebe means to educate, purify, radiate, brighten and enhance. She reflects the purest light of love and wisdom in all living things.

PERSONIFICATION
Symbolising bright intellect, Phoebe personifies the psychic sense of claircognisance, which is clear psychic knowing and intuitive prediction. Her name signifies brightness — as in light, but also intelligence. She is a multidimensional goddess representing the feminine cycles of maiden, mother and grandmother. As a titaness, Phoebe is often portrayed in her wise woman or crone aspect.

TOTEMS
The moon and lightning are Phoebe's main symbols. Lightning strikes symbolise 'a-ha' moments, insights and spiritual awakenings. She is also often seen with a

little she-bear, in lieu of her granddaughter, Artemis. The bear signifies a grandmother's love and protection.

ROOTS

In ancient Greek mythology, Phoebe is grandmother to the sun god Apollo, queen of the crossroads Hecate, and maiden goddess Artemis. Her legacy birthed a long lineage of well-known Hellenic deities. Phoebe was the leading spirit guide of the third Oracle of Delphi, a legacy she in turn gifted to her grandson, Apollo. She inherited this great honour from the goddess of justice and divine order, Themis. Ancient lunar temples are amongst the ruins of ancient Greece.

FOLKLORE

As a titaness, Phoebe is one of the divine children born to Uranus, Father Sky, and Gaia, Mother Earth. Her children have the magical traits of alchemy, prophecy, purification and the superpower to control light.

MOON-HONOURING TRADITIONS

In the ancient Greek temples, a high priestess would begin by holding up a ceremonial vase to the moon. Entering a trance-like state through meditation and ecstatic dancing, she would invite the moon divinity to enter her body temple and speak through her. This ritual was known as 'drawing down the moon'.

41. WISDOM

I share my sage words of insight.

MOONLIT CODEWORDS

Advise, Uphold, Reassure

MOONBEAM INSIGHT

You are being called to realise your goddess-given potential! Goddess Phoebe and her animal totem, the bear, inspire you to trust your natural instincts and reframe any limiting beliefs that are dimming your light. It is your time to stand tall and face life's pressures, fears and uncertainty without apprehension. Your higher self is preparing you for a position of leadership — if only in your own life.

Like Phoebe, the wise woman of the moon, people often seek your astute counsel as your comforting words reassure them with hope and cast-iron certainty. In times of struggle and chaos, you are a leading light and role model illuminating the way for others to follow. Kindness twinkles from your eyes and creates a spark of magic that lights up even the darkest night.

Spiritual wisdom is your understanding that comes from your unfathomable connection to yourself and universal consciousness. It is the ability to see beyond the physical and to understand the interconnectedness of all things. It does not mean that you are picture-perfect, it means that you are imperfectly perfect.

Your age, experience and inborn awareness gives you a unique insight to the situation at hand and supports your sound advice. Your laughter lines, scars and wrinkles are beauty spots of wisdom, so wear them with pride. Your crown of knowledge radiates clear psychic insights and profound inner knowing.

Shine your torch of brainpower and emotional intelligence to enlighten your sphere with the light of good judgement.

Walk your talk by upholding your standards, ethics and values of unity to live a congruent and synchronised existence. Powerfully soft, your empathy, understanding and compassionate elegance soothes the souls of those around you. Your integrity and conviction create a ripple of truth and assurance through everyone you meet.

MOON GUIDE: PHOEBE

The name Phoebe, loosely translates to mean 'pure, prophet, shining or bright'. In Greek mythology, she is the wise and loving grandmother of the sun god Apollo, moon goddess Artemis and shadow queen Hecate. Some say she gave a spiritual voice to the Oracle of Delphi in ancient Greece for some time.

MOON PHASE: BALSAMIC MOON

As the ending stage in the lunation cycle, the Balsamic Moon is the monthly 'sleep time'. Instinct and intuition are high during this final phase. This shrinking moon is a slim crescent, 45 degrees behind the sun.

BALSAMIC MOON RITUAL

Make time and space in your evening ritual to reflect on some of the wisdom gained from your day. This may be meaningful quotes, insights, lessons learnt and shared knowledge. Whatever it is, make it meaningful to you. You may wish to journal on your findings, dreams and visions to find deeper meaning.

WISDOM SPELL CHANT

Oh, grandmother moon, titaness of magic and wisdom, ensure my words are powerful and that I use them wisely. Brightest of blessings, surround me this night, open my intuitive light and might. When the world all around me turns dark, it is through your guidance that I tap into my light. May it be done.

ARTIST PROSE

Through ages time of cosmic lives
Realised in wintered worlds
Unashamed in beauty's grace on charms of counsel's calm,
Of magics wise in wilds unfold through empress ways in mind,
Of ease and sage in seers of two and one
For spirals twist in crested fare in grand of far of sight

Twilight's shade of moon and ground in slumbered wakes in strength
Thine gentle beasts of dreaming doors betwixt and bridges bold
Forbearing hearts of mercy's sooth restores to worldly hold
Sele's nite through fortunes dusk exist through all for you ...

42. INTELLECT

I trust my inner knowing.

MOONLIT CODEWORDS

Inquire, Foreknow, Understand

MOONBEAM INSIGHT

Lightning bolts of inspiration and intuitive thoughts are awakening your imagination and thirst for more knowledge. Ask and you shall receive the insights you are seeking.

Open your mind and awaken your claircognisant abilities. Claircognisance or 'clear knowing' is the psychic gift connected to the crown chakra. It is linked with open-mindedness, higher truth and divine guidance. Suddenly, you will just 'know' something without any prior learning. You may be tapping into the source of divine knowledge or your own intuitive knowing, either way your intuition comes to you through your thoughts. As this portal opens, you attain higher levels of consciousness, awareness and a sense of Oneness unity.

Anticipate your next steps intuitively and strategically. When you merge your analytical brain power with your gift of claircognisance, you create opportunities that lead to endless blessings. Emotional intelligence blended with practical logic is a great combination.

As a truth seeker and spiritual academic, you enjoy the pursuit of self-discovery. You are on a lifelong search for knowledge, wisdom, growth and purpose. It all begins with curious wonder and deciding what you want to explore further.

Your desire for exploration and intuitive understanding keeps everything far more interesting. It isn't just about observing and gaining knowledge, it's about sightseeing the world. A spirited search opens your eyes to the remarkable curiosities of creation. Not everything can be learnt from books; life experience expands your mind to endless possibilities. The real world is an infinite source of learning. While formal education and training has its place, it is not the be all and end all. You are being called to trust in your intuition, higher awareness and innate abilities to learn from the world around you.

MOON GUIDE: PHOEBE

Phoebe is the ancient Greek titan goddess of bright intellect. She has a great mind and a big heart. She is a lunar deity associated with prophecy, specifically the shining light and wisdom that Greeks attributed to the gift of psychic prediction.

MOON PHASE: THIRD QUARTER MOON

The Third Quarter Moon is a time of mindful reflection and introspection. This energy is often sensed as a resistance of two forces: anxious overthinking versus a calm inner knowing. Surrender to the conscious calm within to find inner peace.

THIRD QUARTER MOON RITUAL

Fill your mind with inspirational books, podcasts, guided meditations, mindfulness exercises, puzzles, crosswords, philosophy, positive affirmations or whatever else stimulates your brain. Integrate 10–15 minutes a day to inspire your mind with thought-provoking insights.

INTELLECT SPELL CHANT

I declare to the moon: living a conscious, high-vibe life strengthens my relationship with my wiser self and connection to the divine mind. May it be done in the luminous light of wisdom.

ARTIST PROSE

Radiance bright at third and fore
Through shards of fire realms, they slice
Be hearts and flow in flight
Through glimmers of moon of glinted spears
Lanced vims of spirited drawn and sent
Through blood and fire white heat it knows
From strike and observance marked
Distilled to stars in heavenly palms
Cores' lightning knack is you …

43. CYCLE

I skyrocket from one round to the next.

MOONLIT CODEWORDS

Attract, Repel, Shift

MOONBEAM INSIGHT

You have the power to manifest anything you wish! Love, money, your perfect home, a dream job — the opportunities are endless. It requires you to trust the process, stay positive, believe and have faith in action.

Tap into and align with the moon to amplify your manifestations and craft magic. Each phase of the moon's cycle has a distinct symbolic and spiritual meaning that aligns to the cycle of creation: conception, birth, life, death and rebirth.

Aligning to the moon's cycles means connecting to the energy of expansion, retrieval, healing, growth, intuition and wisdom. When you harmonise your life with the phases of the moon, you bring awareness to the patterns within your body, mind, heart and spirit — the rhythm of life within you. As you attune yourself to her essence, it has a powerful effect on your life.

To manifest, you must intentionally reflect, act and live in a way that ultimately attracts what you desire. The fresh energy of the New Moon is a divine time to contemplate a new project, set intentions, plant seeds, make wishes and get super clear on your steps forward to harnessing your dreams. The Waxing or 'Mounting' Moon is a time for action and forward momentum.

The Full or 'Blossoming' Moon is a time of completion, fruitfulness, shifting and transformation when the seeds from the New Moon come into bloom. Expect vivid dreams, increased intuition and synchronicity around this amplified time. Emotions may run high, so practise self-care during this period. The Waning or 'Dwindling' Moon is a time to look inwards, reflect and tweak your plan ahead of the next lunar cycle.

It is your time to weave your magic and create miracles with the perpetual cycle of the moon.

MOON GUIDE: PHOEBE

Titaness Phoebe typifies the light force, rhythms and energy of the moon. Her link to the moon is synonymous with enlightening or shining wisdom out to those that seek her guidance. As a titaness and colossal power, she is the personification of greater elements and cosmic forces in the universe.

MOON PHASE: ALL MOON PHASES

The perpetual rotation of the moon indicates the unending cycle of creation. Each moon phase has unique qualities and spiritual significance, and when united, the entire moon sequence denotes coming together, culmination and completion.

ALL MOON PHASES RITUAL

When your energy is expansive, you feel light, optimistic, happy, peaceful, hopeful and alive. When your energy is contracted, you feel introspective, reflective, sensitive or reserved. Check in with your body temple. It will intuitively communicate to you which energy you are in. Sense what that energy feels like in your body and reflect on the best way to nurture and nourish yourself at this time.

CYCLE SPELL CHANT

I flow, grow and glow with Phoebe's ever-changing Moon. My wisdom shines from the inside out. I dance to the rhythm of her pulsating moon drum. May her moonlight shine upon me in the dead of night.

ARTIST PROSE

Through core of self thine portal pulls
To lead a cosmic rise
Eonian lights of stardust trails
Brilliance is alight
Hands of heart and Soul of tides
Through night and day eternal now unite

In stillness wakes ember-ed flared
In vastness turns the spirit
Of ether's song and rhythms call
The One ignites your stars ...

44. REFLECTION

*I gain a new perspective about
a bewildering situation.*

MOONLIT CODEWORDS

INTUIT, PREDICT, INTERPRET

MOONBEAM INSIGHT

There is a current matter that is mystifying you. Titaness Phoebe inspires you to go within your own inner oracle to seek the answers. She will encircle and hold space for you to dive deep into your well of wisdom and give this matter the serious thought and consideration it needs.

A clear intention aligns the answers to your specific questions. Start with a topic in mind and trust the reflections that come into view. Ponder on the calm inward musings that bring a sense of clarity to you; here you'll find a trustworthy source of knowledge.

Intuitive awareness conveys clear guidance, whereas incessant worry creates chaos and confusion. The difference between a psychic message and trepidation is the way it is communicated to you. Intuition is conscious calm, a strong sense of perception, not fear wrapped up in limiting beliefs or conditioning. Take a breather, get still, centre yourself and surrender to the wise one within you.

Your psychic expansion is being accelerated at present. You are a visionary that can foresee and foreknow the future. Follow the magical clues to find the path of least resistance. This mystical trail will lead you to higher dimensions of existence and greater psychic clarity. Intuitively construe the deeper meaning of these signs to make them relevant and beneficial to you.

Reflection is the cornerstone of spiritual growth. Selfdevotional practices like meditation are enhancing your connection to the Divine. Expanding your energy means you grow as a person. Allow yourself to receive more experiences in your life that fill you with joy and start living a more fulfilling and healthier life, inside and out.

MOON GUIDE: PHOEBE

Known as the 'Lady of the Sky and Mysteries', titaness Phoebe embodies the mystical powers of flight, the skill to conjure a silver light and the ability to attract abundance and repel obstacles.

MOON PHASE: GIBBOUS MOON

The Waxing ('Swelling') Gibbous Moon is a time for reflection and expansion, and to ponder on the life lessons, insights and internal growth you've gained so far. You may also need to pivot and plan ahead throughout this expansive phase.

GIBBOUS MOON RITUAL

Self-reflection is about looking back with an open mind to grow and expand on past actions taken. This silent meditation conjures clarity. Find a tranquil spot to get still, breathe and centre yourself. Set your intention or ask your questions and allow the messages to flood your psyche. Afterwards, journal the answers.

REFLECTION SPELL CHANT

Lady of Mysteries, shine your silver light on me, clear and bright. The moons of change do glow, the waters of wisdom do flow, the seeds of love do grow. May it be so.

ARTIST PROSE

Augmenting moon heightened wise stood fast in cycles growth
In portals realmed and echoes seen reflections move beyond
Upon the stars and ripples made in mirrors discerning sight
Guides mystic lunar stardust falls in thoughtful swells
In ancient veils farsighted seer of timeless sounds fly forth
Telling scry of shadowed bear and nighted wolf divined
Becharmed by self-passed visage known enchanted paths unfurl
Of self and self of ageless unbound eye
Pooled of liquid knowledge gained and one
For you are you, eternal bound entranced in journeys light …

ABOUT THE AUTHOR

Suzy is a modern mystic, moon lover and star gazer. As an internationally award-winning psychic medium, Suzy has guided thousands of people worldwide with her psychic insights and healing messages. She is also a celebrated author, speaker and intuitive coach. Today, Suzy uses her psychic gifts to gently guide, inspire and teach other souls to nurture their inborn wisdom and live a more intuitive, conscious and heart-filled life. Her creative imaginings are dedicated to weaving mystical rituals into the mundane of everyday life.

Suzy has travelled the globe to explore ancient spiritual sites, moon temples and natural wonders of the world. At these sacred shrines, amongst the beauty of nature and under the rays of the moon, Suzy connected with lunar divinities to bring forth spiritual inspiration and guidance.

With Portuguese and Celtic ancestral lineage, Suzy honours

her rich heritage in her soulful offerings where possible, while also ensuring there is a wide range of diversity that represents the incredible beauty found across the world. In this way, she hopes to inspire Oneness unity, understanding, empathy and equity for all.

Born in Canberra, Australia, Suzy is a proud matriarch, mama and grandmother who wears her wise-elder crown with overflowing pride, love and grace.

I have always felt a deep soul connection and alignment with the moon. I answered the call to honour her beauty and grace, many moons ago when I was a small child fascinated with the glittery night sky. Now in the sage season of my life, I have found the wisdom of age and a depth of understanding that is a beautiful blessing.

In the creation of this deck, I have brought together bright past-life memories, ancient remembrances and divine mysteries channelled from a long ancestry of lunar divinities scattered all over the globe. It's a humbling privilege and an honour to dedicate this luminous offering to the moon deities and the long line of wayshowers who paved the way for modern-day mystics. May the lunar mysteries of the Moon Temple Oracle expand your intuitive senses, mysticism, wonder and manifestation magic.

In love, grace and gratitude,
— Suzy

JOIN THE TEMPLE

The Temple of Intuition with Suzy is a free online space to share, enrich and fine-tune your intuition. It is a thoughtful, collaborative and open-hearted community of sensitive, spiritual souls dedicated to intuitive growth and soul expansion.

To find out more about joining *The Temple of Intuition* with Suzy Cherub, visit: **www.suzycherub.com**

ABOUT THE ARTIST

Goddesses, angels, spirits and beings from the In-between inspire Laila Savolainen's intuitive, open-hearted and magical artworks. She has studied and taught art therapy, counselling, energy healing and shamanic works. Laila's creations are portals to elemental temples, dream-lit realms and places far within your imagination.

The prolific bodies of art that I have been blessed to create depict but a moment, a glimpse into the realms I venture through and the offering that I witness. I have been, and continue to be, blessed to walk beside and dance with the trailblazing wayshowers, the soulful creative authors as we co-create. Every piece manifested is imbued with the vastness and intent, the magical depth of the unseen and the eternal love that is for us all.

— Laila

FULL MOON

The Full Moon shines in the night sky
A silver orb of beauty and grace

She is the goddess of the tides and cycles
The ruler of the dark and the hidden

She watches over us with her gentle gaze
She guides us through our dreams and intuitions

She inspires us with her creativity and magic
She blesses us with her love and compassion

She is the Full Moon, the mother of mysteries
She is the Full Moon, the source of mysteries

ALSO AVAILABLE FROM BLUE ANGEL PUBLISHING®

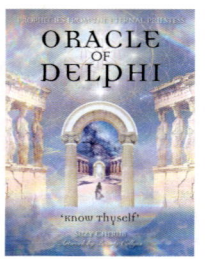

ORACLE OF DELPHI
Prophecies from the Eternal Priestess

SUZY CHERUB
ARTWORK BY BRIARLY COLLYNS

Here, on the threshold of wisdom, you can commune with ancient seers, reclaim miracles and free the future. Here, your questions invite guidance, magic and activations. Here, you can experience a remembering that brings you home to the temple within. This exquisite oracle set is a portal to clarity and understanding. Shuffle the deck to invoke the eternal priestess, choose your cards and welcome wonder, healing visions and sacred empowerment.

May the mysteries of the oracle open your intuitive senses, self-awareness and inner mystic.
—*Suzy Cherub*

44 CARDS + 176-PAGE GUIDEBOOK.
ISBN: 978-1-922573-75-9

ALSO AVAILABLE FROM BLUE ANGEL PUBLISHING®

STAR TEMPLE ORACLE

SUZY CHERUB
ARTWORK BY LAILA SAVOLAINEN

Embody your sacred feminine powers and receive interstellar guidance with this glistening oracle from author, speaker and intuitive coach Suzy Cherub. The ancient wisdom of the Pleiades is weaved together with present-day mysticism to bring you uplifting and relevant insight.

Star Temple Oracle has been birthed to support your learning, creativity, awareness, and growth. Connect with the eternal knowing of the stars and let your intuition flow.

44 CARDS + 104-PAGE GUIDEBOOK.
ISBN: 978-1-925538-87-8

ALSO AVAILABLE FROM BLUE ANGEL PUBLISHING®

FAERY TEMPLE ORACLE
Wisdom and Wonder to Empower Your Faery Spirit

SUZY CHERUB
ARTWORK BY CHRISTINE KARRON

With a sprinkle of possibility, a shimmer of starshine and a whisper of wonder, faery magic is ready to ripple through your world, clearing pathways, releasing limitation and imbuing your heart with clarity, purpose and understanding.

Earthy, visionary and resourceful, the faeries are wise and fearless companions. This gorgeous 44-card set is a portal into their enchanting world of inspiration, insight and delight. Seek answers and discover a sanctuary where wisdom is packaged with joy, love and fortuitous opportunity. The spirited imagery and salient messages from faery sages will help you work with the elements to attract blessings, synchronicity and fulfilment in all realms of your life.

44 CARDS + 120-PAGE GUIDEBOOK.
ISBN: 978-0-648746-87-4

ALSO AVAILABLE FROM BLUE ANGEL PUBLISHING®

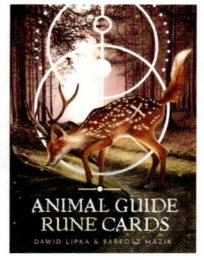

Animal Guide Rune Cards

Dawid Lipka and Bartosz Mazik

Embark on a magical journey as you unlock the wisdom of nature and ancient Norse runes with the *Animal Guide Rune Cards*. This captivating deck weaves together the potent symbolism of foxdeers and owls, bats and badgers, merging the power of the animal kingdom with the esoteric mysteries of runic lore.

Discover the profound and practical insights offered by each of the 25 strikingly illustrated cards and accompanying messages, illuminating every aspect of your life, from relationships to health to career choices. The comprehensive guidebook also includes instructions for creating spellbinding runic talismans and reveals the connections between the runes and tarot, astrology and the chakras. Immerse yourself in the wisdom of the runes and delve into the mythic and cultural philosophy they embody.

Divine your destiny by journeying into the enchanting realm of the Elder Futhark, allowing your animal guides to lead you every step of the way.

25 CARDS + 288-PAGE GUIDEBOOK.
ISBN: 978-1-922574-06-0

For more information on this
or any Blue Angel Publishing release,
please visit our website at:

WWW.BLUEANGELONLINE.COM